A Fair Share of Tax

Lotta Björklund Larsen

A Fair Share of Tax

A Fiscal Anthropology of Contemporary Sweden

Lotta Björklund Larsen
Department of Thematic Studies:
Technology and Social Change
Linköping University, Linköping, Sweden

ISBN 978-3-319-88840-8   ISBN 978-3-319-69772-7   (eBook)
https://doi.org/10.1007/978-3-319-69772-7

Cover illustration: Cover pattern © Melisa Hasan

Printed on acid-free paper

This Palgrave Macmillan imprint is published by Springer Nature
The registered company is Springer International Publishing AG
The registered company address is: Gewerbestrasse 11, 6330 Cham, Switzerland

To Niels

PREFACE

Why do people pay tax? And why do they avoid doing so? There are many disciplines that try to answer these questions—economics, law, accounting, psychology. They use a wide variety of methods and come up with a similarly diverse array of solutions and theories which revenue authorities apply more or less successfully. Yet tax research is not only a contested field; taxation is for most nations and states a necessity for providing funds that finance infrastructure and services for their citizens.

This book adds to the literature on tax compliance by proposing an anthropological perspective, honing in on the reciprocal relations that tax, as with any exchange, can be seen to create. The book is based on ethnographic encounters—being and speaking with taxpayers, tax cheaters and tax collectors.

Fellow anthropologists have often wondered about my choice of field as there are so many exciting issues of human existence to delve into and exotic places where those issues can be investigated. Such collegial comments may qualify me, a fiscal anthropologist, for a gold membership into what Susan Leigh Star coined the 'Society of People Interested in Boring Things'. Yes, taxes can be utterly boring, as can many, many other subjects. But if we think about taxes as forging social relationships, the perspective changes. Taxes finance governmental infrastructure, defence and services for its citizens; in many countries taxes make up one of a citizen's largest, if not the largest, economic relation to anybody. All citizens (supposedly) pay taxes and all (supposedly) benefit from them. In this light, tax collection in practice has an impact on how taxpayers view their relationship with the state and ultimately with other citizens. This is a holistic view of taxation, a view that intimately connects the spheres we call economy and society. This view on tax compliance changes our focus from legal explanations and economic quantifications to descriptions of the type of reciprocal relations that taxes and tax collection entail. As John Locke stated centuries ago, taxes open up issues about democracy and reciprocity. Here it is the latter that is in focus, although democracy plays a role as well.

In this book I delve into taxation as creating relationships of various sorts, and I focus on the taxpayer's perspective. Taxation is made possible by many things; the focus here is on the relations it creates between people, and between people and their state. I argue that in order to understand tax compliance and tax cheating, we have to look beyond law, psychological experiments and surveys to include tax collectors and taxpayers' practices. What do they actually do? What are their views on taxation, in their own words? I explore the view of taxes as citizens' explicit economic relation to the state and implicit economic relation to all other compatriots. Such a view brings us straight to the core of economic anthropology. I end the book with some thoughts about how to build and increase tax compliance if we are to take the creation of reciprocal relations through taxation seriously.

Reciprocity is an old concept and many have advised me to think about other concepts instead. Yet the way I hear Swedes discussing why they pay tax and why they avoid doing so includes varieties of relations and expectations that I cannot find a better word for than reciprocity. This book is thus an amalgamation of several research projects; about the Swedish Tax Agency and about a group of Swedes' avoidance of paying tax. In particular I draw on Chaps. 6 and 7 of my dissertation *Illegal yet Licit: Justifying Informal Purchases of Work in Contemporary Sweden* (2010). There are many quotes from the ethnographic interviews I conducted during my dissertation fieldwork, yet they appear in a different light when contrasted with the views and writings of the Swedish Tax Agency as they aim to make Swedes comply. When I write about the Swedish Tax Agency, I use plural—them. This is to acknowledge employees' voices, opinions and reflections about the society and the citizens they are set to tax. The plural also reflects that there are contrasting views within the Swedish Tax Agency.

I am grateful for the encouragement and discussion about various aspects of this subject—reciprocity's importance in understanding tax compliance—with colleagues inside and outside academia. I call them colleagues because of our common interest in tax compliance issues. In particular I want to mention Mats Andersson, Benedicte Brögger, Nimmo Elmi, Hans Gribnau, Åsa Gunnarsson, Ulf Johannesson, Ingrid Melbi, Emer Mulligan, Johan Nilsson, Lynne Oats, Susanna Wanander and Roger Persson Österman. I am also grateful for comments from the seminar groups at Tema T, Linköping University, where ideas for this book have been presented. Last but not least, Pat Baxter made sure that my message got across. Thank you.

Funding from the European Union's Horizon 2020 research and innovation programme 2014–18, grant agreement No. FairTax 649439 allowed me to write this book, and Riksbankens Jubileumsfond generously provided funding to publish it 'open access' thus making it available to all people interested in why we pay tax. Sustainable tax compliance illustrates, after all, the universal human capacity to give, to receive and to give again.

Department of Thematic Studies: Lotta Björklund Larsen
Technology and Social Change
Linköping University, Linköping, Sweden

Contents

About the Book

In this book I argue that in order to understand why we pay tax—tax compliance—as well as why we avoid doing so, we have to look beyond legal changes, psychological experiments, economic results, the organization of revenue collection and all actors' practices in society's tax arena and study the type of relations, and expectations, that taxpaying is seen to create in society. In this quest, returning to Marcel Mauss and his analysis of the gift and its resulting relations will help us understand this. I want to direct our gaze onto the concept of reciprocity, which is often proposed as an explanation in tax compliance research, and explore its diverse meanings and implications.

CHAPTER 1

Exchanges Create Relations

Abstract There are numerous explanations for why we pay tax, an important aspect being the relations, and expectations, that taxpaying is seen to create. This chapter revisits various research traditions on tax compliance and proposes four different ways in which it addresses reciprocity: *tit-for-tat*, *copy-cat*, *fair share* and *equality*. Sweden, a 'modern' welfare state, has a well-esteemed tax collecting agency that has worked long and deliberately to enhance its standing in society. Despite the agency being liked, tax avoidance is also going on. This ethnography travels full circle around seemingly opposing actors on the Swedish tax arena, at the Swedish Tax Agency and among a group of tax-avoiding Swedes, listening to their stories and justifications—allowing for a thorough understanding of reciprocal relations invoked by carrying out taxation.

Keywords Reciprocity in tax compliance research • Thinking *with* reciprocity • Ethnography of taxation and tax avoidance

> Those who exchange presents with one another
> Remain friends the longest
> If things turn out successfully (Mauss 2002 [1990]: 2)

Thus ends the forty-first stanza in *Hávamál*, one of the many poems in the Scandinavian *Edda*.

© The Author(s) 2018
L. Björklund Larsen, *A Fair Share of Tax*,
https://doi.org/10.1007/978-3-319-69772-7_1

Friends certainly exchange presents, but they do so much more in order to remain friends; especially if they want to remain friends for a long, long time—perhaps even for life. This is also the case if we think more broadly about presents than the occasional birthday gift and the bottle of wine brought for dinner, and extend our thinking to friendship as a helping hand in need or a listening ear when there are things to tell. Yet then comes the third line—'if things turn out successfully'. There are thus not only two 'friends' here, two people who exchange presents in the broadest sense possible, but an externality. Two people, even two friends, cannot exchange gifts in a vacuum. There are other things that can happen which have a potential impact on the relationship.

There is more about such relationships in *Hávamál*. The forty-sixth stanza ends with

> Presents given in return must be similar to
> Those received (ibid.)

Aha… we are looking for an equilibrium. There cannot be any old countergift, but it has to be similar to the initial gift. And finally, in the 145th stanza, we are reminded that exchanging gifts demands courtesy; there is even a hint towards modesty. Yet the reflections in *Hávamál* about exchanging gifts never lose their focus on balancing the relationship.

> It is better not to beg [ask for something]
> Than to sacrifice too much [to the gods]:
> A present given always expects one in return.
> It is better not to bring any offering
> Than to spend too much on it (ibid.: 2–3).[1]

Let the words linger. These poems were compiled and written down in the thirteenth century and they contain histories from the earliest of Viking times. The stories in the *Edda* are from a very different time; they are part mythology and part stories about values, beliefs and livelihoods. They are also the main source of what we know about Norse mythology. The *Edda*, a collection of sagas from medieval Iceland, provides some eternal truths, and this ancient poem in particular still speaks to us about how relations are created by exchanging things, telling us that such exchanges have to be carefully made if the relationship is to remain 'successful'.

I use these stanzas to direct you in space and time; geographically to the north of the globe where Vikings resided, specifically to Sweden, and more specifically again to the country's contemporary tax collection system and the avoidance of such payments. The *Edda* lines about people exchanging and their resulting moral implication are also part of the introduction to the seminal book *The Gift*. Written by French sociologist Marcel Mauss and published in 1925, it is a slim book about the universal human capacity to give, to receive and to give again. It grants us examples from all over the world of how people make exchanges and the relations these exchanges create; how people reciprocate. It proposes that by exchanging, by offering a gift as it were, society is made possible. It suggests that to exchange 'things', and thus create relations, is an eternal human propensity.[2]

Yet *The Gift* is probably the most inappropriately named book in social science (Hart 2007) as it discusses so much more than the altruistic transfer of a good. Expanding the gift to a more ubiquitous exchange such as market transaction, trade, barter, swap, transfer and even theft can see such exchanges as creating some sort of relationship. And what if we think about taxes in those terms? As a type of exchange that also creates relationships?

Taxation is a hotly debated topic in most countries, and citizens all over the world pay—and avoid paying—various taxes and fees to their government. Taxes finance infrastructure, defence and welfare for the supposed benefit of all citizens. Most countries have an elaborate and organized tax structure to collect tax revenue and transfer it to institutions in order to pay for various public needs and government functions. As taxation is instituted by laws, failing to declare or to pay tax, as well as evading or resisting taxation, is usually also a punishable offence.

Citizens, therefore, are more or less forced to pay various taxes but also live in the society where the revenue is collected and allocated.[3] This creates the expectation that they will get something back; but what will be given is the subject of much consideration and debate. Taxes and the collection of tax are in their broadest definition what politics is all about: who should pay, how much is needed, and how and on whom the state should spend the money that is collected from its citizens and other taxpayers. Yet this is not the primary issue at stake here—my focus is on the expectations that taxation create. Regardless of what we pay tax on, there is usually some sort of expectation that we will get something for the fees, taxes and excise paid to the governing body. If we give something, we also expect to

get something back, regardless of whom we pay. To give something creates a relationship, and the focus in this book is on the relations that taxes
and taxation, as a process of collecting revenue, create.

In this book I argue that in order to understand why we pay tax—that
is, why we accept tax compliance—as well as why we avoid doing so, we
have to look beyond legal changes, psychological experiments, economic
results, the organization of revenue collection and all actors' practices in
society's tax arena and study the type of relations, and expectations, that
taxpaying is seen to create in society. In this quest, returning to Marcel
Mauss and his analysis of the gift and its resulting relations will help us
understand this. I want to direct our gaze onto the concept of reciprocity,
which is often proposed as an explanation in tax compliance research, and
explore its diverse meanings and implications.

First, taking reciprocity seriously means that we have to expand the
view of reciprocity as a dyadic relation between two exchangers to include
other citizens/members of society which in matters of taxation is often
synonymous with the state. I shall argue that similar types of expectation
to those that exist between exchangers reside in the relationship that citizens as taxpayers have with the state. Although exchanges between inhabitants and state are vast even from a daily perspective, impossible to
quantify or account for, and immensely complicated in a welfare state, we
will see that there is a residual sense of a reciprocal relationship. From a
resident's perspective does thinking about taxes in reciprocal terms also
make for demands on the state? Indeed, does paying taxes have an impact
on one's expectations of what society should provide?

Second, thinking about taxation as giving something draws our attention to the balancing that goes on in society. Paying tax means creating
and maintaining different types of societal relationship and acquiring an
identity in such relationships; giving too much—or receiving too much for
that matter—has, according to Mauss, implications for the status that one
has in society. What is the impact of a given tax system, its redistributive
effect and the resulting reciprocal relations it creates on one's societal status, one's group in society, and one's society vis-à-vis other societies?

Third, I will direct your attention to the actual giving and taking—and
the order in which this comes—to explain how cheating by taxpayers can
be justified and thus made legitimate (at least in their own eyes).

Viewing taxes as a citizen's explicit economic relation to the state and
implicit relation to all other citizens brings us straight to the core of economic anthropology. Our focus thus changes from legal explanations and

economic quantification to the type of reciprocal relations that taxes and tax collection entail.[4] Fiscal anthropology starts out from this perspective and frames this book. With this approach, we explore the view of taxation as the citizen's relationship to the state and to all compatriots, based on ethnographic examples from Sweden. The book concludes by raising the gaze from Sweden in order to propose a number of considerations regarding reciprocity that societies have to deal with—if they are aiming to increase tax compliance.

'I tell you why I buy work off the books. This family has paid far too much to the state already,' says a former neighbour. I heard a number of people expressing themselves in similar terms when they were explaining why they, and other Swedes, engage in informal transactions. Expressed in those terms, can such purchases be seen as a response to a feeling of having contributed too much to the state? To regard taxation in a modern democracy such as Sweden from a relational point of view casts a more nuanced light on Swedes' propensity to cheat with taxes. Life is not so simple that their motives for purchasing informal work are purely economic, (im)moral or continue the way 'we have always exchanged', but it reflects the view that 'in the course of the day, we enter into an immensely wide array of exchange relationships, with complex relations between them' (Slater 2002: 237).

In the following you will get to know more about my former neighbour as well as many other Swedes. There are the *Limningers*, a group of middle-aged people who went to the same school as I did. You will learn about their explanations and justifications for complying with and avoiding taxation, focusing on the reciprocal aspects—there were many other types of justification (Björklund Larsen 2010). *Limningers* explain their different strategies and experiences of informal exchanges for avoiding tax, but also what makes them comply. Then there are the employees at the Swedish Tax Agency, hereafter referred to as the Agency. These analysts, managers, legal experts and tax collectors are more or less aware of citizens', such the Limningers', various justifications and strategies. We will thus also receive the collectors' perspective on what makes up the relatively high tax compliance that Swedish society is said to have; a level of compliance that is made possible by the Agency's careful and detailed handling of an all-encompassing tax law. This book thus goes full circle around the issue of Swedish taxation, listening to both tax collectors' and citizens' explanations in an ethnographic light.

All informants' real names are anonymized. This was particularly important regarding the *Limningers*, who after all spoke about illegal exchanges. Any information about surroundings, life stories and family conditions has been slightly altered in order not to reveal any possible connections between statements and specific informants. Occupations have been changed as well, but to something with similar status in Swedish society as well as similar access to informal exchanges. All interviews with informants, both *Limningers* and those at the Agency, including the many meetings I attended at the Agency, have been transcribed word for word. In what follows, all informants' quotes are literal translations into English.

DEFINING TAXATION

Taxation serves many purposes and the ingenuity in finding new ways to tax citizens is simply amazing. Probing into definitions of taxation tells us more about this variety. The *Encyclopaedia Britannica* states in its entry on taxation: 'imposition of compulsory levies on individuals or entities by governments. Taxes are levied in almost every nation of the world, primarily to raise revenue for government expenditures, although they serve other purposes as well' (www.britannica.com). It continues:

> [D]uring the 19th century the prevalent idea was that taxes should serve mainly to finance the government. In earlier times, and again today, governments have utilized taxation for other than merely fiscal purposes. One useful way to view the purpose of taxation, attributable to American economist Richard A. Musgrave, is to distinguish between objectives of resource allocation, income redistribution, and economic stability. (Ibid.)

States use taxation to attract business, change consumption patterns, redirect investments, create incentives for sustainable choices and so on— 'tax legislation for non-fiscal goals is an integral part of government policy' (Gribnau 2015). Already we can see that taxes serve other purposes than merely to provide government, regions, municipalities or other public institutions with income. Increased taxes can redirect consumption by making certain products and services more expensive, thereby counteracting alcohol and tobacco use, for example. They play a role in improving the environment, for example by subsidizing sustainable energy or by diminishing or abolishing taxes altogether on certain products and services in order to make them more attractive. Income redistribution has the objective of reducing inequalities of wealth and income among the citizens—or increasing them—or helping certain categories of citizens, for example students, expectant parents or retired people, who are in need during a particular period of their life. Finally, taxes can influence investments in order to provide economic stability or collaborate with other economic policies in order to promote the solid and sound economic development of a given society.

Some nations levy a flat percentage rate of taxation on personal annual income, others on a scale based on annual income amounts; some have marginal taxes where the amount paid increases with income levels; and a few countries impose almost no taxation at all, or a very low tax rate for certain areas of taxation. Some countries levy tax both on corporate income and dividends; this is often referred to as double taxation, as the individual shareholder(s) receiving this payment from a company will also be levied some tax on dividends included in personal income.

A distinction is usually made between direct and indirect taxes. Direct taxes are those whose burden cannot be shifted from one taxpayer to another; one example is an employee's income tax that is directly calculated on and levied from her/his salary. Indirect taxes are levied by an intermediary, who is different from the person who bears the ultimate economic burden of such tax. Although such taxes cannot be directed to specific taxpayers, they are usually seen to have the largest impact on low-income earners who have, *ceteris paribus*, less money to spend on consumption than do high-income earners.

The definition of tax is slightly different in the *Swedish National Encyclopaedia* as it is directly related to the Swedish context: to its historical development, the type of taxes, that it is based in Sweden's democratic institutions, and is clearly connected to the welfare state. The definition says (my translation):

> Tax is a statutory payment to the public without direct reciprocity. The constitution stipulates that only the people's representation, the Riksdag, has the right to decide on tax. In the modern welfare state, the need for tax revenue has grown strongly. Important taxes are government and municipal income taxes, VAT, excise taxes on alcohol, tobacco and energy and social security contributions. (www.ne.se, accessed 1.4.2017)

Note that taxation is a payment 'without direct reciprocity'. We will get back to this. Taxes [in Sweden] are levied by the state as well as by county councils and municipalities. VAT, excise taxes and social security contributions go to the state while income tax is paid to both state and county councils and municipalities. Regardless of recipient or type of tax, all are collected by one governmental body—the Swedish Tax Agency, *Skatteverket*.

Researchers suggest a multitude of reasons why taxpayers pay up—or avoid doing so. The usual remedies mostly go hand in hand with researching disciplines: legal scholars want to improve the law (Lodin 2007); economists emphasize economic incitements and punishments (Allingham and Sandmo 1972; Lindbeck et al. 1999; Schneider and Enste 2002; Engström and Holmlund 2006); social interactions theory (Gordon 1989; Fortin et al. 2007) brings in social aspects into economic models explaining tax evasion (Alm 2012: 14); economic psychology tests various social norms in experiments (Kirchler 2007) and political scientists applies for example institutional theory (Steinmo 1996).

Tax compliance research also shows that it is affected by (social and personal) norms such as those regarding procedural justice, trust, belief in the legitimacy of the government, reciprocity, altruism and identification with the group. Studies indicate that certain demographic factors such as age, gender and education correlate with views about tax (Kornhauser 2007; cf. San Juan 2013). To say the least, there are many issues to investigate concerning our willingness to pay.

There are also those who apply a qualitative approach in investigating what people actually do when they collect or pay tax—or avoid doing so. In a social constructivist approach, the description of the practices at the Danish tax authority allows us to understand how tax compliance is effected in a variety of settings. This is always a laborious feat involving the participation of many actors: not only auditors and taxpayers but also the knowledge, technology, rules and regulation that provide active enforcement of these various people (Boll 2011, 2014a, b). These studies show that the state's role in making sure taxpayers comply does not reside (only) inside the state but it is also the effect of a heterogeneous assembly of other actors and practices (Boll 2011: 225). It is a perspective of what tax collectors do when they make taxpayers comply (apparently voluntarily). For other ethnographic studies of tax authorities see Pierluigi De Rosa (2014) on the Italian Tax Authority and Gregory Rawlings and Valerie Braithwaite (2003) on Australians' perspective of their Taxation Office). Similar approaches have been applied by studying tax professionals in US multinational enterprises, showing that these experts have a subtle yet powerful impact on the wider institutional tax environment (Mulligan and Oats 2015); in discussions about taxes on freelancers' online forums (Oats and Onu 2016); or in a famous UK case of presumed tax avoidance, where it is shown how the various contenders—tax authority, tax professionals, taxpayers—negotiate both their actions and motives regarding tax regulatory practices (Gracia and Oats 2012). Such qualitative approaches make for 'thick descriptions' of both actors and contexts, with the aim of increasing our understanding of why people behave in certain ways (cf. Geertz 1973). Taxpaying is after all very different in the USA, in Sweden and in Kenya, just to mention a few examples.

What is underscored here is not only how the multitude of disciplines regard tax compliance; the issue is also the methodology used within each discipline (which of course varies). A valid question to keep in mind is *how* we get to know about how various taxes and taxation methods are understood and accepted by the people paying and collecting them. What can be known and what are the implications of such knowledge? Taking reciprocity seriously also means thinking about how we get to know about reciprocal relations.

RECIPROCITY

Now we have defined taxation, what about reciprocity—what is it? The word comes from Latin via French, *reciprocité*. It denotes the status of a relation or an action between people, countries or organizations that is governed by 'a mutual exchange of commercial or other privileges'. There is a mutuality to a reciprocal relationship.

Looking up 'reciprocity' on Wikipedia provides a bewildering number of definitions and usages across many disciplines, which might say more about the contemporary academic tendency to create—borrow—terms across disciplines in order to create 'new' concepts. Compare this with the entry in the *Encyclopaedia Britannica* from 1988, which only provides a short description referring to the concept's application in international trade agreements. It is defined as 'mutual concessions in tariff rates, quotas, or other commercial restrictions' between countries who sign such agreements. The logical extension is a full customs union, where the encyclopaedia's entry refers to what is now referred to as the European Union (EU). According to an anthropological textbook, reciprocity is '[t]he mutual exchange or obligation. More generally, the relation between people in an economic system, the obligations they have towards each other in such a system, or the practices they engage in in relation to one another' (Barnard and Spencer 1996: 619). In this fiscal anthropological perspective, this is where I put my main emphasis.

It needs to be underscored that reciprocity is just one of many, many issues that need to be understood if we want to increase tax compliance in society. This book takes reciprocity seriously, yet does not undermine all the other important facets that make taxpayers comply. The multitude of disciplinary research methods and insights does not mean that the research is undertaken in separate silos; despite criticism of particular disciplines by others, there is also much sharing of insights regarding what makes people comply with tax regulations—and avoid them. This book examines *all* types of research that have addressed the issues of relation building through taxation—reciprocity—and their impact on tax compliance. I want to take account of explanations of what can be said to be reciprocal relations based on ethnographic data and an anthropological approach. This is a book about how the relationships that taxation creates are described from all stakeholders' points of view. Reciprocity is thus not taken as a given phenomenon, but is brought into focus in my interpretation through documents, stories, anecdotes and reflections from Swedes in various capacities.

WHY SWEDEN?

So why Sweden and what can we learn from this relatively small nation? Sweden provides an interesting case when looking at taxation and tax compliance for several reasons.

First, the Swedish welfare state has often been and still is considered a role model (e.g. Svallfors 1995), even if many other countries provide the same level of welfare but perhaps in different configurations. Sweden was a poor and underdeveloped country that grew wealthy during the last century. It escaped both world wars, and industrialization based mainly on rich resources of iron ore and forestry developed without interruption. This growing wealth was the source for simultaneous development of the welfare state as industry and state cooperated and grew for the benefit of each other (e.g. de Swaan 1988; Rothstein 1992; Allvin 2004). The welfare state developed mostly, but not exclusively, under a social democrat government. One political idea during this development was *Folkhemmet*, literally the People's Home, where all citizens would feel equal (Frykman and Hansen 2009: 80) and where no one would be dependent on or abused by any other (Lewin 2008: 30). The soil for such development was fertile as Sweden was never feudal; the inherent idea of equality might have earlier historical roots than twentieth-century social engineering (Berggren and Trägårdh 2006: 52). One of the consequences of *Folkhemmet* was an evening out of differences in income levels (Bennich-Björkman 2008: 47), and this enhanced equalized standing between citizens, simultaneously provided a foundation for welfare policies through the taxation of personal income from work. However, the *Folkhemmet* as a place of equality where class adherence would not matter and social mobility might have been the highest in the world is said to be fading away in a global world of increasing income inequalities (Rosenberg 2013: 183).

Second, Swedes pay among the highest income tax rates in the world (Denmark is usually considered to be at the very top). VAT rates are also very high in Sweden by international comparison, although corporate tax rates are more moderate and comparable to those of similar countries. But if we are to take the reciprocal element in tax compliance seriously, Sweden provides a very interesting case because of these high rates. People pay quite a lot and without making too much fuss about it, but they also—as we will see—believe/perceive that they get quite a lot for their taxes. But as in any nation, there are many, many ways to avoid taxation, and citizens also partake quite actively in more or less elaborate tax avoidance—usually on the margins.

The main funding for the Swedish welfare state derives from taxes, of which the largest amount originates from wages or salaries (approximately two-thirds of the total tax collection).[5] More or less all people that receive income pay taxes, a sum that in total substantiates most of the governments revenue. The reiterative endeavour of building governmental institutions that include most of a population has created a sense of the collective. The contemporary Swedish welfare state can be seen to be the product of collectivization *and* of corporatist efforts (Rothstein 1992; Rosenberg 2013). This effort has resulted in a modern society that is shaped in its most intimate aspects by this process (Rothstein 1992: 11). Regardless of alternating political regimes in Scandinavia, social expenditure continued to rise during the twentieth century, continuously reinforcing the welfare state and at the same time creating 'a strategic environment in which people operate as calculating entrepreneurs' (de Swaan 1988: 229). This is argued to include both experts who get their income from providing services as well as claimants of these services. Giving and taking is in this view a practice informed by self-interest, although simultaneously contributing to the 'collectivist' construction of the welfare state.

Corporations also support an important stepping stone in the building of Swedish welfare state. Early on in the social democratic regime, there was a tacit agreement that the state should not interfere in relations between employer organizations on the one hand and labour unions on the other, making for a corporatist agreement between these two parties. This is the very foundation of the Swedish model: peace between opponents on the labour market, economic growth and the encompassing welfare state (Rosenberg 2013: 160). Although these opponents, employers and labour unions, had different views on the level of taxation, there was in essence an agreement about the structure.[6]

Third, the revenue-collecting Agency has a very particular standing, being one of the most revered governmental agencies among the Swedish population today. Much tax research would consider it strange that people pay their taxes without much fuss. In fact, 69 per cent of Swedes think the Agency performs its duties well and only 5 per cent have negative views of this authority (Holmberg and Tryggvason 2014: 11). This has not always been the case (Stridh and Wittberg 2015; cf. Björklund Larsen 2017: 1–3), but the Agency has worked diligently to change its way of working. It mediates the application of law and fulfils the orders of government, but also strives vigorously to be seen as legitimate in its practices by the citizens (e.g. Skatteverket 2008, 2012; Björklund Larsen 2017, Chap. 2). Acquiring legitimacy is achieved by applying strategies such as being serviceable, collecting the 'right'—not the maximum—tax and minimizing taxpayer errors. As the Agency states: 'it should be easy to do it right and difficult to err' (Skatteverket 2014).

Citizens have repeatedly confirmed the Agency's standing in surveys since 2006 (Arkhede and Holmberg 2015: 22, 24). Therefore, the Agency not only enforces laws and regulations but pay attention to the impact they have (e.g. Skatteverket 2007, 2008, 2012). I attended many meetings where this standing was confirmed, following thoughtful and insightful employees who seriously try to engage with how society around them sees taxation (Björklund Larsen 2017). There is a continuous discussion among analysts and managers about the challenges that such an Agency meets in fulfilling its task of collecting the 'right' tax.

Fourth, Sweden is seen as a 'modern society'. According to the World Value Survey's measurements of cultural values, a survey that describes variations in such values among approximately seventy nationalities, Sweden has a very particular position (Ingelhart 2006).[7] If we are to believe such surveys, Swedes are both very rational but also very unlikely to worry about survival issues; they trust both their government and fel low citizens. The World Value Survey argues that there is a continuous inclination towards these values, a fact that makes Sweden appear to be a modern and somewhat trend-setting nation. The question is whether other countries will go in the same direction.

Fifth, it can be argued that Swedes have a direct relation to the state according to both rights and responsibilities, in a type of social contract that is influenced by Rousseau's ideas (Berggren and Trägårdh 2006: 53). Rousseau's contract between citizen and state demands that the individual subject himself to a common will, an idea incorporated in the welfare state (ibid.: 50). Individuals are thus emancipated but also alienated from hierarchical relations, and the welfare state will protect them so that no one has to depend on family or others in order to survive (ibid.: 49), situations in which an individual can easily be taken advantage of. Henrik Berggren and Lars Trägårdh paint a picture of a society of people with equal rights, no one worth more than another. So if one were to attempt to characterize Swedes, they may be described as not wanting to be dependent on each other and thus desiring of symmetrical relations (cf. Daun 2005). They are considered highly individualistic, but at the same time they have a lot of trust in the orderly and rationally organized Swedish state. This seeming paradox is defined as 'statist individualism'. Statist individualism comes out of a deeply rooted and popular democratic view within society, based on the Jante Law rather than originating in people's natural rights of universal equality (Berggren and Trägårdh 2006: 43). This 'law' originates in a book about Danish (and, more broadly, Scandinavian) culture written by Aksel Sandemose in 1933, *A Fugitive Crosses his Tracks* (English translation 1936). It consists of ten commandments, all determined by jealousy, habits and ways of living in a small town where contacts with the larger world are restricted and social change slow. In common parlance, the Jante Law is unwritten but carries the message that 'thou should not regard thyself as better than any other'. The historical origin of statist individualism is thus argued to go further back than the social engineering of the Social Democratic welfare state during the nineteenth century (ibid.: 49 ff). It has its background in the history of a nation which was never feudal, where common men have been relatively free in a comparative perspective and where ideas that no one is superior to anyone else are deeply rooted.

Understanding the Relationship
between Society and Tax

In order to understand any society and its political life, one of the best starting points is taxation (Schumpeter 1954). Schumpeter proposed the view that a nation's fiscal organization and history have an enormous influence on how a nation develops (Musgrave 1992: 90). Taxation is in Schumpeter's view the very foundation of the state; if there is no income the state is unable to act. Unless the state is socialistic, with everything owned by the state and thus no taxation being needed, taxation has to come from citizens and other entities outside the public sector. Taxation both divides the private from the public, but simultaneously connects these spheres.

Although Schumpeter combined a view on taxation from historical, financial and sociological perspectives with his practical experience of having served as a finance minister in the Austrian Republic after the First World War, he took mainly a macro-perspective. Income taxation should be understood as being at the nexus of a nation's economy, the formation of the state governing this nation and the expectations—the values—held by citizens peopling this state (cf. Musgrave 1992: 11). Proceeding to inquire as to why people pay tax to such a state, I turn to the 'new fiscal sociology' as advocated by John Campbell (1993) and especially by Isaac Martin et al. (2009). In their research agenda they move the focus to society's informal institutions such as family, friendships, work and trust, and investigate among other things the determinants of taxpayer consent.

If we take seriously reciprocal relationships as an outcome of taxation, one could argue that reciprocity must be even more pertinent in states with high tax rates—that is, where a large part of the price of a private purchase, as well as net personal income, is tax. There are different explanations for why high tax rates have been accepted: because of war, as some historical research has indicated (e.g. Campbell 1993: 167), but also because of the building of a welfare state. High taxes can be said to originate in the organizational strength of societal groups and of the institutional structure of the state (ibid.: 168). Swedes actually became more content with taxation from 1960 to 1980 despite the almost exponential increase in tax pressure during the period (Hadenius 1985: 362). Research showed that it was not taxation per se that Swedes appreciated, but the benefits provided by it. They got something in return for the taxes paid.

Fieldwork: Ethnography of Swedes' Views on Taxation

Following Schumpeter, this book takes ethnographic examples from Sweden in order to illuminate how taxation is made possible by highlighting issues and contexts where reciprocity is played out. In what follows you will visit many coffee shops, workplaces and homes to have *fika* (coffee and cake) with informants,[8] as well as following me through the corridors of the headquarters of the Agency to attend meetings and interviews. Through these visits, my aim is to illuminate how taxation is made possible in one of the nations with the highest tax 'burden' in the world; albeit one where there does not seem to be so much questioning of taxation.

The data for this book comes from two anthropological studies. In the following I describe the fieldwork but also contextualize the acquired information in time and space.

The first study addressed how informal purchases of work—*svart arbete*/black work—in Sweden are justified among a group of middle-aged Swedes (Björklund Larsen 2010). These purchases, which look like any other bought work, are said to make up a substantial part of the economy in contemporary society, but are strictly legally speaking tax cheating exchanges. Such exchanges are hidden and subject to ethical, moral, economic and practical considerations, and although politically challenged they seem to exist everywhere.

The societal phenomenon I studied was one that Swedes are constantly exposed to and come into contact with in everyday life—through the media and people's constant engagement with the question. Recurring indignation in headlines caught my attention and a never-ending stream of examples of *svart arbete* in known and new guises was overheard—fragments of conversations at the supermarket, when watching children's soccer games and even when listening to discussions about how to keep within the legal framework at the Scout corps when the youngsters wanted to earn extra income for a trip to a Jamboree in England. There are even humorous advertisements about buying *svart* in newspapers, relating to stylish leather sofas, or the tip cup at a coffee-shop counter that says *svarta pengar*.

This study was done in 2003–4 and society around us has changed; the everyday, and justifiable, purchases of *svart arbete* seem less frequent today. What we hear about now instead are examples of despicable abuses of *svart arbete*: of immigrants without working permits working for less than nothing; of out-sourcing chains of cleaning services where the invoicing provider is completely clean—white—but where subcontractors are hired in an increasingly dirty chain of informal yet organized work and tax swindles; about contractors within the building industry who deliberately dupe the state through avoiding VAT.

Simultaneously, there is also increased awareness among corporations and politicians that everybody should take responsibility for sharing the expenses of the state. The former Social Democratic Party leader Mona Sahlin famously stated: '[I]f you are a Social Democrat, then you think it is cool to pay taxes. Tax is for me the finest notion of what politics is all about.' This is perhaps not surprising; but Per Schlingman, former chief strategist to the Swedish Conservative Party, also agreed with her (although many years later), writing: 'To contribute to the commons is right and responsible and to be unsolidaric is limp.'

Such statements could be written off as political propaganda, yet tax experts within corporations confirm these views. The Chief Financial Officer (CFO) of one of Sweden's largest corporations said in an interview:

> There is an increased focus on tax compliance; sometimes the tone in the media—and also coming from certain politicians—is that you should pay more than you ought to (according to his interpretation of the law)—just because we are one of the big, well-known corporations. Then it is difficult to find the right level, both in relation to the public media and in relation to the taxation rules. Yet our decision-making has changed. A decade ago we could consider buying an unprofitable corporation (whose deficits could then be used as a deduction from profits). Such a strategy is unthinkable today; now we only consider the business-related issues in imaginable acquisitions.

The Agency has spearheaded similar thinking. Former Director General Ingemar Hansson argued that tax morals have been changing in Swedish society. In one article he described the resignation by the chairman of one of Sweden's largest pension funds, AMF—a pension fund jointly owned by the Swedish Trade Union Confederation (LO) and employers, via the Confederation of Swedish Enterprises—owing to his tax planning scheme as a change in tax morals. Through his private company the chairman had used a so-called Peru scheme, and the revelation that he had done so made for his resignation from the AMF. The Peru scheme was based on a bilateral tax agreement from the 1960s between Peru and Sweden that made it possible to transfer profits from a Swedish company to a Peruvian one, with such profits only being taxed at 4.1 per cent. In a decision by *Högsta Förvaltningsdomstolen*, the Supreme Administrative Court, in March 2012, such profit transfers were ruled illegal. If the activity generating the profit had taken place in Sweden, taxation on such profits would have been applied there. Hansson argued that this resignation was a sign that taxpayers in general are today less forgiving of tax planning: to pay tax is to show a concern for the society in which the taxpayer works and operates (Hansson 2011; cf. Björklund Larsen 2016).

These small snippets from the public debate illustrate the growing awareness about complying with tax. There are obviously manifold causes and reasons for this change, including the increased automatization and digitalization of taxation issues especially at the level of revenue authorities.

For example, I would suggest that it is more difficult to justify the everyday purchase of *svart arbete* owing to the introduction of ROT (*reparationer, ombyggnad, tillbyggnad*—repairs, refurbishing, attachments) and RUT (*renhållning, underhåll, tvätt*—cleaning, maintenance, laundry) subsidies (in 2007), and the Agency's smart implementation and simplification of using such deductions since then. ROT subsidies have been used now and then to boost the building industry in times of a slack economy. This is an old trick in the finance department's toolkit as the building industry sector is seen as one of the initiators of economic growth in society. ROT subsidies could be used for certain types of reconstruction work in private homes with tax deductions up to a given amount, but also as a way to lessen the propensity for undocumented work. ROT is almost unanimously supported by both politicians and citizens whereas RUT has been subject to an infected political debate addressing issues of gender, inequality and abuse (Gavanas and Calleman 2013). RUT is also a play on words taken from earlier established ROT deductions: Rut is a female name, and women traditionally perform the cleaning in Sweden.

These subsidies make various home services considerably cheaper and the Agency has made it very simple to use them. When ROT and RUT were initially implemented, the reporting and repayment system was cumbersome: one had to pay for the non-deducted services, make sure the provider had registered with the Agency, save all the receipts, add them up, fill in forms at the end of the year with the details of the various providers and finally wait to get a refund several months later—and over a year after the first of the purchases was made. Today these subsidized service deductions are already in place on the prepopulated yearly tax return form (for more about the annual tax return, see Chap. 2). Such automatization and simplification of what was once an unwieldy administrative task makes for increased acceptance of such services.

At the time of my fieldwork about how informal purchases of work were made and justified, I had certain concerns (for more detail about this, see Björklund Larsen 2010, Chap. 2). First, it seemed that trust between the informant and me was a necessary ingredient for the interviews to be successful as just posing a question of why and how a person buys services informally could imply accusing this person of illegal actions. This could obviously provide all sorts of replies—anger, contempt, shame but mainly silence. The informant and I have to have some sort of relation in order to address such questions.

Second, more or less every Swede seemed to be involved. Whatever questions you asked regarding informal purchases of work, the answers all seemed to confirm that you could always find what you were looking for (e.g. Portes et al. 1989: 298, Williams and Windebank 1998: 83). Research has also shown that *svart arbete* is exchanged amongst people of all social categories, ages and political opinions (e.g. Svallfors 1995). Amongst the *Limningers*, some buy a lot of *svart*, most take the occasional opportunity to do so and a few refrain from it as much as possible. Thus, looking for an ethnographic field I wanted a group of people who had something in common yet lived and acted in different realms of society. Inspired by Sherry Ortner's fieldwork on class in the USA (cf. Ortner 2003), I contacted the group of people with whom I graduated from school in 1976 in a place I call *Limninge*. This is a small town in the west of Sweden; hence this group of former classmates is thus collectively referred to as *Limningers*. As we will see, they provide many different views on what ought to be subject to tax and what should not. They represent diverse social categories and live and work in many different ways in cities, townships, and the countryside throughout the south of Sweden. In the midst of life, they share a long experience of work and life and the memory of our teenage years at the same school I attended. This shared memory provided a platform for trust where illegal yet licit purchases were revealed in ethnographic interviews (Davies 1999: 95–6). Although, these interviews are more than ten years old, I hear the same arguments repeated in contemporary Sweden, although less frequently now.

The second study derives from three years of fieldwork at the Agency where I followed a risk assessment project taking place in its analysis department (Björklund Larsen 2013, 2017). This project developed quite naturally from the previous work on *svart arbete*. In the first study, there was more than one informant who intriguingly posed the question 'what is *svart arbete*—in reality?' This question was hard to give a direct reply to, as the concept does not legally exist. Recognizing that it was the Agency that has the difficult task of interpreting and implementing the law, I became interested in how they drew the line between what on the one hand could be considered a helping hand and on the other a clearly taxable market trade.

The latest tax reform is from 1991 and made for substantial changes.[9] Among them, it was stated that all exchanges deemed as having value ought to be subject to tax assessment. This is regardless of whether the recompense consists of money, a service in return or material objects. In theory, the bartering of services compares with exchanges recompensed in cash, and neither the extent of the exchanges nor the relationship between them ought to be considered for tax exemption (Björklund Larsen 2017). This implies that not only is income from (self-)employment taxable, but also that any other exchanges having value that take place between citizens ought to be subject for tax assessment. My interest in how the Agency drew the line here turned into a more specific question about the type of knowledge they apply in interpreting such fickle laws, especially given the Agency's good standing in Swedish society. The analysts thought my questions were interesting, and I was invited to follow this risk assessment project ethnographically.

The project developed into one of the largest risk assessments ever undertaken by the Agency and I was with the project from its initiation, during research meetings, at a random audit control and a research consultancy, and at most meetings when the Agency was informed about its progress. It took three years to finish the report, and interestingly enough the results were deemed too sensitive to be published publicly. Insights from the report were obviously used at the Agency, and new work practices were implemented in the control systems and daily practical audits the following year.

Being with this risk assessment project for three years allows me to bring insights into the broader workings of the Agency and to many aspects of how they interpret the law, how they understand society, how they perform taxation and the relationships they aim to create with taxpayers. Presentations for Agency management about the resulting risk assessment report repeated many previous questions about taxpayers' behaviour.

Why do taxpayers make errors? Who are these taxpayers? What measures is it possible to reinforce in order to minimize the problems? The discussions that followed were therefore old issues dressed in new clothes. 'It is an interesting subject [why taxpayers make errors] as it pinpoints many issues that are at stake [for the Agency],' said one manager. This fieldwork helps us to understand issues that the Agency considers in its daily work of creating compliance.

Part of the risk assessment project was a random audit control that was of particular interest. A total of 400 entrepreneurs' cost deductions was audited in detail, and the outcome was unexpected. Not only were certain deductions more prevalent than originally thought among a specific category of taxpayers, but questions were also raised about the interpretation of the law in practice. Could such cost deductions even be controlled? Such insights are difficult to communicate, as they contradict not only the message that all taxpayers pay their fair share, but also that the Agency can apply the law equitably and fairly.

Although brief, this book will travel full circle around seemingly opposing actors in the Swedish tax arena. We will get to know why citizens pay taxes from a reciprocal perspective—from people who pay, evade and avoid tax as well as those who collect them.

We know that the behaviour of other taxpayers is important for taxpayers' willingness to comply with tax regulations—or rather the *perception* that all other taxpayers pay. Many propose reciprocity as one of the explanations. But how is reciprocity explained, invoked, used? When we actually talk about tax compliance in relation to reciprocity, what do we mean?

There are a number of models that apply notions of fairness, altruism, reciprocity, trust, social norms, guilt, shame and morality in various capacities. In this book I will take up the notion of reciprocity, engaging with it from an ethnographic perspective to relay how groups of Swedes discuss such relations. They seldom talk about reciprocity per se, but I am interested in how they articulate the relationship invoked to other taxpayers by the act of having paid, paying and the intention of paying tax—or explicitly avoiding doing so. The ethnographic perspective means taking individuals seriously; both taxpayers and tax professionals (which is a term I will apply to all people working professionally, yet outside academia, with taxation in Sweden). Tax professionals are here mainly employees in various capacities—analysts, managers and so on—at the Agency, but also tax advisors at large auditing firms, CFOs and other employees working with taxation at corporations, and various other experts working with tax issues at interest organizations. I therefore use the plural—them—when I write about the Agency. This is acknowledging the employees' voices, opinions and reflections about society and the citizens they are set to tax.

When informants speak about why taxes ought to be paid, or avoided, I do not judge but purely listen in. This especially concerns the *Limningers*, as their explanations are neither poor excuses nor whitewashes; instead they illustrate how people in their justifications equalize or balance perceived outstanding obligations, both to the state and to other people in society. It is time to take reciprocity seriously. Here I explore it with ethnographic examples from contemporary Sweden in order to add to our understanding of what makes people comply with taxation.

In the following I will go through different strands of research that address reciprocity as an important aspect of what informs our knowledge of tax compliance—not forgetting avoidance strategies. This short recap will also point to the issue of methodology and show that it matters.

RESEARCH ON WHY WE PAY TAX

Research disciplines addressing tax compliance mostly display a benevolent approach and a genuine interest in sharing insights from one discipline and applying them to other methods, analytical approaches and ways of reasoning. For example, economists apply a sense of moral or social obligation to models of economic reasoning (cf. Andreoni et al. 1998: 819). Therefore what follows are excerpts from research in these various disciplines that proposes reciprocity as an explanatory factor.

Reciprocity is said to be one of the explanatory norms in research on tax compliance and evasion (Alm 2012: 12); it is even proposed that the concept will be one of five research directions governing future research on tax evasion (ibid.: 27). James Alm acknowledges the many insights made over the last forty years, yet also articulates many outstanding issues that are yet to be investigated, dug into more deeply or explored; for example, the correlation between issues that are found to explain tax evasion. Thus economics is not the only source of theoretical explanations. I find Alm's proposed five future research strands inspiring. First, he probes for more theories but simultaneously warns us that such theories are contextual; they will probably not 'fit' all individuals and not even the same individual on every occasion. Models are, as always, an *attempt* to understand and explain reality. In this book (mostly inspired by anthropological theory about economic behaviours), I bow to Alm's second proposal that such theories will come mainly from outside mainstream economics. Alm's widely cited article is inspired by the work of George Akerlof and Rachel Kranton (2000) and Akerlof and Robert Shiller (2009), and proposes a view of the economy where 'alternative perspectives' on human behaviour play a role in explaining economic decision-making—tax evasion—in the labour arena. Third, the focus ought to shift from the modelling of individual behaviour to the aggregation of individuals. One implication according to Alm is that we should consider other taxes as well as individual income tax, another is the fact of belonging to groups always has implications on individual behaviour, regardless of whether you call these groups culture, society, organizations or whatever. Alm recognizes that the same individual does not always behave in the same way. Just because I am a woman with an academic degree, who lives in an apartment in a large urban environment and bikes to work does not mean I make the same economic decision every time. I however challenge Alm's fourth proposal, of further laboratory experiments, and his fifth proposal, of controlled field experiments, as ways forward to test proposed theories. Instead I suggest that researchers should direct their gaze to people's lived experiences. There is a world out there, filled with ample examples of people living and acting under a multitude of tax regimes around the globe. In addition to clinical experiments where the modelling of experiments and the posing of questions allows us to construe people's behaviour, we have to ask about and observe what people do and engage with in their everyday life.

The goal for an economist is, of course, to find tools to measure the level of tax compliance or tax evasion and also to identify and explain factors that have an impact. From these, a proposed control of such factors can be suggested. As an anthropologist, it is my modest contribution to present various notions and definitions of reciprocity, beyond the usage of economic and legal literature, in order to contribute to the '"full house" of strategies to measure, explain, and control the "full house" of behaviors and motivations' (Alm 2012: 28).

Economists have, for example, tested taxpayers' willingness to comply applying theories of pro-social behaviour, where the argument is that people are more inclined to do what others do. In this vein of tax compliance research, reciprocity means that if other taxpayers pay their due taxes, other citizens would also feel obliged to pay. And the opposite also applies: in a context where many avoid paying tax, the propensity for the individual taxpayer to do the same is greater (Rabin 1998; Fehr and Falk 2002). A valid follow-up task would be to make a distinction between copycats and those who comply because there will be more in the treasure chest to share in the society we belong to collectively. Challenging *which* reciprocity is in play makes for different policies to address non-compliance.

If taxation is considered a social action, the behaviour of individual taxpayers will be strongly influenced by that of others (Frey and Torgler 2007). Frey and Torgler maintain that there is a strong correlation between conditional cooperation of the individual and the extent of tax morale or of tax evasion. It is noteworthy that this research is based on attitudinal data from the European Value Survey: thirty countries were sampled and at least 1000 individuals in each country responded. The following statement, for example, was proposed, offering answers on the scale of 1 (never justified) to 4 (always justified): *Cheating on tax payments if you get the chance.* The responses were correlated with six variables seen to have an impact on societal tax morale: an individual's voice and accountability, society's political stability and absence of violence, government effectiveness, regulatory quality, rule of law and control of corruption. Frey and Torgler thus stress the importance of political institutions in each of the societies they study, implying that taxpayers' money has been spent on institutions that make for a democratic society and good collective governmental services. The quality of those matters on how citizens interact socially; for example, if others pay taxes so will I. By defining tax morale in this way, Frey and Torgler simultaneously address reciprocity on an institutional level and the perceived expectations of other taxpayers to comply with democratic institutions.

In social behavioural/psychological models reciprocity in relation to tax compliance is dichotomized in various ways; as either strong–weak, negative–positive or horizontal–vertical.

Diving into these dichotomies, we can view reciprocity broadly speaking as people's tendency to respond 'nicely' to actions they are in favour of and 'nastily' to those actions deemed unfavourable for them. If reciprocal feelings are strong, it means that people favour the relationship with others instead of pursuing their own self-interest, whereas if reciprocity is weak the self-interested notions have the upper hand within the proposed exchange (Guala 2012). Negative reciprocity is the result of getting something for nothing, for example stealing (cf. Sahlins 1972), whereas positive reciprocity enforces a common expectation of a positive contribution in return (for something given) regardless if it is in the form of a gift, a service, a compliment or a loan. Finally, the vertical variety of reciprocity illustrates the relationship between the public sector and taxpayers (Alm et al. 1993; Frey and Torgler 2007; Bazart and Bonein 2014) and the horizontal variety is the relationship between taxpayers themselves. These relationships have been studied as separate entities in studies of unfairness in taxation, yet as they are both potential sources of unfairness they ought to be studied in tandem (Schnellenbach 2010; Bazart and Bonein 2014).

Reciprocal behaviour is always posed as a response to that of other players—perceived, real, imagined. Reciprocity is a disposition to cooperate with others, but also to punish those who cooperate for reasons of self-interest; it is a norm that makes people comply with tax rules. 'Acting under this norm an individual will respond to another's act in the same way in which that person treated him' (Kornhauser 2007: 9). If a person is treated with generosity and kindness, s/he will respond in kind, whereas if treated badly the response will be in the same fashion. The implication of a strong norm of reciprocity is also said to go for taxes: if others are perceived to pay so will I, whereas if no one else complies why would I (ibid.: 7; Slemrod 1992)? Reciprocity thus needs careful nurturing as its impact on tax compliance can go both ways. As we will later see in the *Limningers'* justifications, it becomes quite clear that participating in the informal economy, or in the formal for that matter, is taught. We learn to do certain things, among them how to deal with and respond to taxation.

Another distinction is between how taxpayers' money is collected—the fairness of the fiscal system—and how money is spent once collected. Tax evasion can be justified in terms of government expenditure; if I disagree with government policies—how tax money is spent—it is easier for me to avoid paying up (Andreoni et al. 1998). Survey evidence points to similar findings. If government services are not good enough it is easier to evade taxes (Hanousek and Palda 2004), yet we do not know if this is a justified afterthought stated in surveys (Slemrod 2007) or in interviews (Björklund Larsen 2010). Needless to say, such behaviour is influenced by external circumstances; for example, can more taxation be tolerated in times of warfare (Feldman and Slemrod 2009)?

Reciprocal ideas have been subject to the hypothesis that suggests taxpayers 'cheat' if they perceive that their money is not being well spent (Spicer and Lundstedt 1976; Smith 1992). A classic example of such reasoning is Henry David Thoreau's refusal to pay a poll tax, for which he was eventually put in jail. It has been questioned whether his reason was that the American federal government did not abolish slavery (cf. Andreoni et al. 1998: 851) or if he was registering a protest against the American–Mexican war (http://historyofmassachusetts.org/henry-david-thoreau-arrested-for-nonpayment-of-poll-tax/); the point is that avoiding payment of tax can be, and has been, used as a protest against what taxpayers' money is spent on.

Suggesting the modelling of such behaviour seems futile, yet attempts are many. For example, a model of a dynamic and retrospective analysis of the relationship between government public good provisions, government waste, considerations about fairness and taxpayer compliance was proposed (Pommerehne et al. 1994). In this experiment taxpayers were repeatedly asked to decide how much to pay reflecting on experiences from the previous period. Individuals were less inclined to comply if waste had been perceived to increase and also if the gap between 'optimal public provision' and actual level widened (cf. Cowell 1990; Bordignon 1993). The challenge is how best to include such effects in theoretical or empirical analysis (Andreoni et al. 1998: 852).

For legal scholars, the notion of reciprocity is approached in terms of relationships between legal subjects, for example the legal (asymmetric) relationship between taxpayer and tax administration (Gribnau 2015), but also between the lawgiver and taxpayers (Gribnau 2013); more specifically in terms of communication. Discussing reciprocity in this way draws on philosophical notions in order to achieve a more equal status in the tax arena where counterparties are by definition unequal.

Such a reciprocal relation between in essence two unequal parties means that a fair exchange has to be carefully maintained (Westerman 2014). Reciprocity cannot be presupposed; it is not given. Instead it is asked if the law itself should be presupposed to facilitate reciprocity as a desirable feat. There is a continuous need for legal and political interventions to secure a fair and equitable relation between citizens (ibid. 184).

And not only between citizens: a tax authority is the right hand of the state and has considerable powers to collect revenue and investigate taxpayers' (economic) lives. It is appropriate to ask, as does Hans Gribnau, what the implications for tax compliance are if the communication of tax law is governed by the principle of reciprocity as opposed to law as top-down command (Gribnau 2015)?

For a tax collecting authority, to enforce compliance through reciprocal norms in this sense means that communication has to be on an equal footing; it also implies that taxpayers at the outset have to respect the intention of the law. Leaning on Baruch Spinoza's view of the law means that people by definition obey it and behave according to it; otherwise it cannot be a law. Citizens comply with law even if it conflicts with the moral values they hold; even if the disadvantage of breaking with the moral order is outweighed by the benefits of social order (Gribnau 2015: 196). Taxpayers should not fear the law but respect it for the benefit of societal good. Following this reasoning, it is therefore essential that a tax authority should apply a reciprocal communication when levying taxes. Now, because of the complexity of tax law, there is a lack of legal certainty, and it is up to the tax authority to explain this in a reciprocal, communicative way. This can give rise to unintentional non-compliance—and even over-compliance—resulting in a violation of legal certainty and equality (ibid.: 205–6).

Tax compliance research thus shows a wide range of how reciprocity is applied. Summing up, I see four different ways in which we can speak about reciprocity in tax compliance research.

- The obvious reciprocal relationship is to expect something in return for taxes paid; a *tit-for-tat* relation. I play on the disambiguity between various definitions of tit-for-tat: of earlier definitions of vengeful and negative reciprocal behaviour and the more recent definitions of getting something back. In experiments based on the 'prisoner dilemma game', tit-for-tat strategies are seen to protect the actor from being abused or to make his intent in exchanging crystal clear. The scrutiny is on receiving something in return for what I have given—for my 'payment' (cf. de Waal 2000). I expect something in return for having given/paid my tribute to the state. There are time lags between giving and receiving something in return, and as Mauss pointed out these time lags have implications for the relation created. To establish good relations, there needs to be an appropriate time lag, otherwise it is just any market exchange.
- Reciprocity implies a relationship with others, so that I as a taxpayer do what other taxpayers do in the sense of wanting to behave in a similar way. This is a *copy-cat* relation where the reciprocal content is in doing what others, in a similar position to myself, do. Such reciprocity can be invoked for any human behaviour. It is learning by doing what others do. This way of seeing reciprocity is closely related to the notion that we all pay a fair share.

- Taxpayers comply as they expect others to pay their *fair share*. If we all put what we owe into the same treasure chest, we have all paid. It is the collectivity of providing means for everybody's benefit. Reciprocity is here articulated as the explicit provision of taxes by all other taxpayers in a given society, and the implicit trust that taxes collected will also be distributed equally and fairly.
- Reciprocity in being treated equally—a question of *equality*. Here, scrutiny is directed towards the power of the law and interpretation of the same into rules and regulations. There ought to be a reciprocal relationship despite the fact that there is an uneven distribution of power between the collector of taxes and the providers—the taxpayers. This is not only because of enforcement; tax law is by definition complicated, and the tax authority also has immense powers based on its knowledge of tax law that should not be abused.

These four categories of reciprocity obviously overlap. Wanting something for my tax money does not have to be for my individual benefit, but may indicate that I want such money to be spent on societal issues I value and hold dear. A tit-for-tat expectation can go hand in hand with a feeling that other citizens should receive their fair share and be treated equitably.

Leaning on Alm's suggestion of turning to other disciplines when addressing issues that help us to better understand tax compliance, I will use economic anthropology and especially the work done around and following the *Gift* in order to see what it has to say regarding reciprocal relations. There are a number of insights to be had that draw on descriptions of various types of exchanges and the relations they create. As we will see, there are many types of reciprocal relations invoked when talking about relations created by taxation, at least in the Swedish context. The point is to acknowledge that different types of reciprocity have an impact on tax compliance.

Looking into the many types of exchanges humans engage in and their resulting reciprocal relationships might seem a long walk from the issues of tax compliance, but we will learn something from the relations that exchanges are said to create. After all, recall both the array of explanatory factors proposed by the research on tax compliance above as well as Swedish tax law. To repeat: the latter states that anything with value that is exchanged, regardless of how it is remunerated, ought to be subject to tax.

Choosing which exchanges to tax ought to be subject to careful consideration in order to create voluntary compliance, but also to steer attention towards what citizens ought to get in return for their contributions. Although Sweden is a small and 'exotic' nation in the values its citizens hold, understanding the relations that taxation create in that country ought to be of interest to other nation states—for other tax law legislations.

ANTHROPOLOGY OF ECONOMIC EXCHANGES AND RECIPROCITY

Marcel Mauss regarded gifts as 'total social phenomena' (Mauss 2016: 58), meaning that a gift draws on an immense number of societal aspects and institutions. This one-way transfer of a good creates relations and is thus a way in which social relations within society can be defined. According to Mauss's study, the obligations of the gift are three in number; to give, to receive and to reciprocate—that is, to give again (Mauss 2002 [1990]: 9).

Something given provokes reciprocity in human relationships, thereby complicating them. The recipient feels forced to respond, starting a chain of other exchanges, dispersed with different time intervals that will govern future relations. It is important to underline that the gift does not necessarily start a good relationship; having received something, the recipient can also choose not to respond (Davis 1992: 24, Mauss 2002 [1990]: 17), whereby the relationship will deteriorate or end. Those who give and those who receive might have very different capabilities for reciprocating in terms of an equal relationship. In this way reciprocity can also be exclusive, as those who give much also receive much. 'Apparently, reciprocity is not morally good in and of itself: reciprocal acts do not necessarily lead to a more just or fair society' (Komter 2014: 161). The gift, either altruistically given (Gudeman 2001: 80) if there ever was one (cf. Derrida 1995), or the one meant to create reciprocity, is identified with the contributor, and the gift's intention is thereby real, changing and ambiguous (Davis 1992: 79). A gift offered might at first sight be provided out of sympathy with the recipient, but less noble intentions might be hidden—a quest for attention, blandishment, manipulation or even bribe (Komter 1996: 3).

Reciprocity is a relationship constructed out of exchanging something for something else; it is a mutual obligation people have towards each other following an exchange. Reciprocity has been part of anthropology since anthropologists started to cast their gaze towards how people lived and exchanged; investigating the *economy* if we can set householding, survival and other means of existence apart from people's everyday life. The concept has therefore often been used to address relationships in primitive but also informal and non-market economies.

Reciprocity is the outcome of an array of human exchanges; from altruistic gifts, via market transactions to pure theft, where the exchanged items have been food, services, commodities, land, sacred items and the ultimate gift—the woman (Levi-Strauss 1966: 204). Reciprocity as an explanatory factor has in anthropological literature been applied to many a context: emotions among Swedish civil servants (Graham 2002); everyday sustainability among sugarcane workers in Brazil (L'Estoile 2014); beggars in Rome (Thomassen 2015); US garage sales (Herrmann 1997); and even in the concentration camp of Auschwitz (Narotzky and Moreno 2002), just to mention a very few examples.

One of the examples that Mauss drew on in his book was the *kula* trading system in the Trobriand Islands. Bronislaw Malinowski, a Polish anthropologist educated in England, was stranded there during part of the First World War and had ample time to investigate the economy, the householding and the intricacies of exchange among the Trobrianders. He described the *kula* exchange that took place between islanders when visiting each other. This was a ceremonial exchange, used to create relationships and obligations (Malinowski 1966 [1922]). A giver presented a valuable armband or necklace to his host with much ceremonial brouhaha, showing the more or less discreet pleasure of drawing the recipient into a relationship where the latter needed to provide a countergift. This countergift could not of course be reciprocated directly, but had to be given on a suitable future occasion. Noteworthy is that not all exchanges were considered *kula*—on the contrary, among the Trobrianders it was important to distinguish them from the barters and purchases of everyday necessities.

The quality of things exchanged matters and so does the quantity. The person in society who receives the largest gifts has most status. As s/he must reciprocate, one assumes that s/he has more than what s/he receives, making her/him able to reciprocate with an even bigger gift. If unable to do so, her/his status dwindles. A too large gift, such as almsgiving, degrades the recipient, especially if it is given without expecting a gift back (Mauss 2002 [1990]: 95).

Moving our scrutiny to contemporary Italy, more specifically amongst the *popolino* in Naples,[10] the recipient of many gifts is considered privileged because status in society increases with gifts (Pardo 1996: 154). Many gifts imply that the donor has resources that has been or will be used. There is a fine line between this position and receiving too much without reciprocating: if society considers the reciprocal action to be too slow or not reaching expected levels, esteem will turn into contempt. The recipient's superiority as net provider is no more; instead the reputation of a net receiver is acquired and a status of dependence manifests itself (Cuco i Giner 2000: 315). Pure charity hurts a recipient's pride and his/her status in society diminishes if there is no possibility of reciprocating the gift (Mauss 2002 [1990]: 83). Politics of welfare can simultaneously foster solidarity between society's members but also exclude net receivers, in their own and other's view, as they have no means of reciprocating (Komter 1996: 7).

But what is it that creates the relationship? Is it *what* is given or *who* the giver is? Mauss described the reciprocal relation created by the gift as a spirit, the *hau*, which he borrows from the Maori in New Zealand. This spirit of the gift-giver resides within the thing given and stays with it until reciprocated; 'to accept something from someone is to accept something of his spiritual essence, of his soul' (Mauss 2016: 73). This was criticized by Raymond Firth, who instead showed that this spirit was within the gift given, not with the person who gave it (Firth 1959). There are thus various views of who carries the spirit; whether it is the something that is given which is of importance, or the person who gives it.

The most common exchange in modern society is the market exchange.[11] Both Mauss and Marshall Sahlins in his study of stone-age economics (see below) left this out of their analysis, and the existence of a market transaction in primitive societies is contested. A market transaction was originally defined as being exempt from creating reciprocal relations; it was supposed to be a spot exchange performed through profit maximizing and by unsocial actors (Swedberg 2003), but has in later studies been shown to result in different types of reciprocal relations as well (e.g. Befu 1977; Davis 1992; Offer 1997). I will delve into the market transaction in what follows as it plays a fundamental role in taxation. It is market exchanges that first comes to mind when we think about exchanges subject to tax.

The modern market trade has money as a means of settlement in return for a product. The exchange is usually based on a predefined price. The producer does not have any contact with the consumer, who instead buys from an intermediary via an institutionalized shop. Buying a litre of milk in contemporary Sweden is done from any kiosk, service station, grocery or supermarket and is hardly ever bartered from a person owning a cow. A sweater is purchased on appearance and a book on content, but the consumer identifies the product with the store or the brand and not with the salesperson. If the product is faulty and the consumer complains, the response to the complaint most likely influences the next purchase. If the milk is sour it's poured away, and it's no big deal unless it happens again. If the sweater shrinks or the book has pages missing, it does not live up to expectations. The salesperson is an intermediary with whom to negotiate, but is seldom the direct target of blame. When buying a commodity for money, the spirit of the provider of the gift is gone.

The spirit of the transaction can help explain the quality of the relationship between the counterparts in the exchange, regardless of whether the transaction is a pure gift or a market deal. Talking about spirits within a modern market transaction can sound strange, but there is something beyond the simple exchange of money for a product/commodity. There is a lingering feeling of getting good value for money spent, some sort of spirit residing with the object bought. If what is bought doesn't live up to expectations, doesn't work or fails for some reason, we blame the provider–producer. The thing acquired can be exchanged for a new object, backed up by receipts and warranties and the entire legal structure behind these simple pieces of paper. When exchanging services, there is no object exchanging hands. Thus, the spirit, if we continue to call it thus, of the transaction dwells within the resulting work, even more explicitly with the provider if the work done exceeds our expectations. And the opposite is equally important: poorly done work irritates us. This feeling remains with the work done even after the service has been rectified and the provider and customer ought to be quits.

Even the latter examples demand varying amounts of reciprocity—food is bought at the local grocery to support local industry, a friend's garage is used for car repairs in order to sustain the friendship: it is the repetition of market exchanges that creates relations. Reciprocity can be discussed and defined theoretically, but reality depends on the context (Gregory 1994: 936). Although the self-interest increases with the distance in the relation (Komter 2014: 161), we can see that the accumulation of exchanges creates reciprocal relationships regardless of where the exchange takes place.

Existing social relationships thus create different motivations to recip-rocate even in the market. There is therefore a continuum of reciprocal types depending on the intent behind the exchange.

RECIPROCITY PROLIFERATING

Regardless of whether a transaction is an altruistic gift or a market transac-tion, the resulting reciprocity describes the quality of the relationship between the counterparts involved in the exchange. A reciprocal relation-ship does not imply an immediate repayment. The time between what is given and what is reciprocated is of vital importance. A direct reciprocat-ing return can be experienced as an offence to the existing relationship; in the worst case the relationship will be terminated (Davis 1992: 85; Ledeneva 1998: 167). An immediate return makes the gift into a market transaction, whereas delayed reciprocity makes us hope for a future possi-bility of receiving something if we need it ourselves. One example given is donating blood (Komter 2014). This is a type of indirect reciprocity, where 'I scratch your back, you scratch another person's back and that person scratches mine' (ibid.: 162).

Reciprocity can also be described in terms of debt or obligations. When we receive something, we have to reciprocate in some way; it is how we do this that defines our standing in society. The distinction between different types of moral reasonings when you are in debt, in debt economies (High and Hall 2012), matters to many people. Being in debt makes us focus on the time aspect between what is given and received, although in Holly High's argument it becomes more: debt becomes another type of a total social phenomenon about which we can have diverse moral reasoning.

A seminal way of thinking about reciprocity was proposed in a study of stone-age economies (Sahlins 1972). There were three defined types—'negative', 'balanced', and 'generalized' reciprocity. First, generalized reci-procity is described as mainly taking place within the family. Generalized reciprocity is giving without expecting something in return. These give and take relationships occur between kin or close subjects who have many other social relations than those based on exchanges. Outside the family there is balanced reciprocity, which is the result of exchanges within a community. Also called symmetrical reciprocity, it is more like a transac-tion between neighbours where both parties are believed to benefit in the long run. The return of the given goods or service supposedly takes place at some future date, so the exchange is based on a fair amount of trust and social connectedness. The third and final type of reciprocity is negative, with examples such as theft and barter, where one of the subjects involved in the exchange earns at the expense of the counterpart. This relationship is one of enemies or between strangers. The reciprocal categories are thus related to modes of social organization (house, lineage, village, tribal, intertribal).

Sahlins's work has been criticized. Perhaps it is an 'overstretching of the notion of reciprocity to cover transactions that are clearly not reciprocal at all such as "generalized reciprocity" for sharing and "negative reciprocity" for stealing' (Widlok 2013: 15). Second, the claim that generalized reciprocity always implies close kinship relations does not empirically stand up to the fact that sharing has been observed at times to be indiscriminate in regard to specific kin relations. Sharing may in certain context include everyone present, even 'distant' visitors or anthropologists who are not treated as close kin in other contexts (ibid.: 15–16).

This is an important point, yet almost tautological. In Sahlins's structural analysis, there are set rules for exchanging that depend on existing relations, yet as Thomas Widlok shows such rules are manners or traditions that make for developing relations between people. It is the very notion of sharing with strangers that creates reciprocity. In many societies, it is good manners to behave this way and to be generous, as the generosity will eventually get back to us when we are visiting someone else. It is reciprocal.

So back to the source. Even if Marcel Mauss wrote about the *Gift*, he rarely applied reciprocity as a term and perhaps did not even give it much thought, but rather only applied it to the habit of giving something back for what has been received. However, the discussion in Mauss's book about the gift suggests that 'reciprocal' is more than a practice; it is an obligation, a feeling (MacCormack 1976: 97)—regardless of whether or not we denote it as a spirit. Reciprocity as a concept should therefore be used with greatest caution. MacCormack's critique was aimed at researchers' sloppy distinction between the social phenomenon itself and the usage of the term as a 'tool of analysis' (1976).[12] On the one hand he observed that it is difficult to denote what exactly is happening in an exchange when applying reciprocity as an explanatory concept; if it is used emically describing a custom or if it is a necessity for survival. On the other hand, reciprocity is also used etically to analyse exchanges in certain societies (ibid.: 101).

My critique of tax compliance research as inadequately explaining the type of reciprocity as an explanatory factor could be said to follow Geoffrey MacCormack's path. The point of this book is to show the manifold guises that reciprocity takes in taxation. Reciprocity needs to be recognized in all its different aspects when we think about why people pay tax.

I thus see versions of reciprocity to be the result of most exchanges, regardless of the context in which they take place. Exchanges within the family, with kin, friends and acquaintances, on the so-called market and in politics all create diverse types of reciprocal relations (Graeber 2001; Hart 2007). This view also means that diverse types of exchange are possible with the same counterpart (cf. Callon and Latour 1997), and that the outcome of an exchange does not need to be material or monetary but can also be entirely social (cf. Befu 1977).

Critiques have emphasized that the concept of reciprocity is too diffuse and devoid of the power dimension, and is thus meaningless as a comparative explanatory factor (Graeber 2001: 217). Yet the beauty of Mauss's argument is that it is not definite (cf. Maurer 2016: x). The argument in *The Gift* allows us to think about what the reciprocity existing in the world can entail and to consider that relations matter. Bill Maurer points out in his foreword to the most recent translation of *The Gift* (2016) that Mauss does not provide us with a final argument about the causality of reciprocal relations, but rather sketches what societal possibilities such relations carry with them—and also the implications if we do not make room for reciprocity in society.[13]

This is also the role of *The Gift* in this book. I follow a long tradition of thinking *with* reciprocity, and have outlined above a few of the many thoughts about how we can understand exchanges in terms of reciprocity and especially the type of (reciprocal) relations that taxation create. In the following I want, instead of trying to define what reciprocity is and is not, to think about contemporary Swedish varieties of tax compliance, invoking instances where reciprocity can be said to be at play.

The point is that many different types of exchange and the resulting more or less reciprocal feelings exist side by side in any society. Reciprocity is thus used as the concept describing these relations, not only as the practice of exchanging things for mutual benefit. The act of giving and receiving—exchanging—is not only a 'total social phenomenon' but also a universal human trait. Exchanges might not be *the* origin of society, but can be argued to hold society together (Befu 1977: 255) as they create personal relationships between actors. By exchanging, people create, nurture and maintain relations between each other.

TO SEE TAX AS A GIFT—OR?

So more specifically, what is its role in taxation? Returning to Mauss, at the end of *The Gift* he moved the analysis from historical accounts and 'archaic' societies and indicated implications about what the gift would mean for the then contemporary society (about 100 years ago), when discussions and political initiatives had started to shape at least the contours of a welfare state. His concerns were about what (economic) exchanges do to men's morale, and maybe shared morals (Hart 2007: 481), and thus ultimately how society is politically shaped.[14] Reciprocal exchanges provide the normative foundation on which the welfare state is based as it 'implies a moral regulation of dependencies in a system of rights and responsibilities' (Jacobsson 2006: 21, my translation).

But '[t]axes are not a gift', states Jacques Godbout. He disagrees with Mauss in that a state and the gift 'system' are complementary. The state fulfils its distributive role in two very different ways: first, through complete anonymous indirect or direct monetary transfers; second, as a dispenser of various services: for example, social, health, support, schools. 'The state system tends to make decisions independent of personal relations and characteristics, on the basis of abstract criteria derived from rights' (Godbout and Caille 1998: 61). It is the democratic law that decides who should receive 'gifts' from the state, not by market selection but by a political decision about what the collectivity of citizens should acquire. As we know, this varies greatly between nation-states. From the state's perspective, citizens are both 'taxpayers', providers of revenue, and 'clients', recipients of governmental services. Godbout argues that the phenomenon of the gift is subjective and a potential source of [great] inequality, which is something a state should deter.

I partly agree with Godbout if we take the state's perspective. However, turning to the perspective of the taxpayers—the citizens—and looking at the entire system of taxes and what they provide, taxes can certainly be seen as at least containing reciprocal relations. Taxes have been given—taken is perhaps more appropriate as most taxpayers do not have a choice—but there is clearly an expectation of receiving something in return, of relating to others receiving similar things and also making sure that we all contribute in some way. It is the state in its capacity of democratic institution that decides what will be returned, not as a personal gift but rather to selected categories of citizens.

Therefore, we are interested in the views that citizens—taxpayers—have of the authorities, and the views that authorities have of taxpayers. Ultimately, the latter has to be persuaded to comply with taxation; thus they make the state possible (if the state does not have other income).

'A strong inner feeling of being morally obliged to return the gift is the quintessence of real-life reciprocity' (Komter 2014: 162). So when we as citizens who belong to a certain society pay into a common coffer for financing things that we all ought to benefit from, we simultaneously create expectations of getting something in return while also creating expectations that all other citizens will provide their fair share at some point.

CONCLUSION

The gift carries with it three obligations: to give, to receive and to give again. And this is also what taxes make us do if they should sustain. In our contemporary societies, there is an endless giving and receiving going on with state and with society—every day and in manifold different ways. Against this background it is interesting to explore taxation in terms of reciprocity.

We saw in research about taxation that four different types of reciprocal relation could be identified. First, reciprocity that expects something very explicit in return for taxes paid; a *tit-for-tat* relation. I expect something in return for having given/paid my tribute to the state although, as Mauss stated, obviously time lags between giving and receiving something in return. Second, it implies a relationship with others in the sense of wanting to behave in a similar way. Reciprocity here is a *copy-cat* relationship. Such a reciprocity can be invoked by any human behaviour: it is learning by doing what others do and making sure we do the same thing. This way of seeing reciprocity is closely related to situations where we all pay a *fair share*—the third type—when taxpayers comply because they expect that others will pay their fair share. If we all put what we owe into the same treasure chest, we have all paid. Implicit here is our trust that taxes collected will be distributed evenly. Finally, reciprocity also regards being treated uniformly—it is a question of *equality*. Here scrutiny is directed towards the power of the law and the interpretation of the law through rules and regulations. There ought to be a reciprocal relationship, despite the fact that there is an uneven distribution of power between the collector of taxes and the providers—the taxpayers. This is not only because of enforcement; tax law is by definition complex, and the tax authority has immense powers through its knowledge of tax law, which should not be abused.

What follows is an exploration of the concept of reciprocity played out in different ways in the Swedish tax arena. *Reciprocal relations* are taken seriously, yet they are perceived and imagined relations pronounced by the very actors that deal with taxes in practice—taxpayers and tax collectors. You will meet some of the *Limningers*, a group of middle-aged Swedes, and hear their reasoning about taxes in terms of reciprocity. You will also become acquainted with employees at the Agency in order to hear their views of reciprocity as played out in taxation and how they see the challenges facing Swedish taxpayers in contributing their *fair share*. The book ends with the proposal of a fifth type of reciprocity that has to be considered when understanding tax compliance, taking account of people's propensity to exchange. It is the *quid pro quo* exchange, the common, everyday transaction between people where the state is left out of the deal.

In Chap. 2, *Taxpayers' Relation to their State*, we will deal with taxation as a reciprocal relationship between taxpayers and the state they live in. We will explore taxpayers' perceptions of contributing with taxes, or receiving from the common treasure chest, and what this has do to seeing taxation as part of a reciprocal relation. Chapter 3, *Taxpayer to Taxpayer Relation*, moves the focus to explore the reciprocal relation that taxpayers create among themselves as an implicit result of taxation. As Sweden has a law that says all exchanges have value, regardless of how they are compensated, they ought to be subject to tax assessment. We will see how Swedes exchange in private and how reciprocity is invoked to keep out the state. Chapter 4 highlights the tensions that are created between perceptions of who pays and who receives in society. The focus is on balancing a reciprocal equilibrium. Swedes assess the taxes they pay not only in relation to what they receive, but also in relation to other residents—they compare their contribution with perceptions about what fellow citizens pay and receive. In Chap. 5, I conclude by proposing that the quid pro quo exchange should be included in the array of reciprocal relationships that impact tax compliance. The final take home from all the expectations is that if we are to actively create a legitimate taxation regime, all taxpayers need to contribute.

NOTES

1. I am grateful to Hans Gribnau who directed my attention to this.
2. It could be more. Animals also are known to exchange things, for example chimpanzees (e.g. de Waal 2000) but as monkeys do not pay tax—yet—that is outside the scope of this book.
3. There are many other taxpayers—but the focus in this book is on human individuals and their relation to taxes and taxation.
4. Taxes are, as we saw in the introduction, used for many purposes, and one of these is wealth redistribution. In Karl Polanyi's seminal analysis of the economy, reciprocity was one of three behavioural principles governing primitive economies, drawing on Malinowski's account of exchanges in the Trobriand isles (1966 [1922]: 59). Reciprocity was described as a symmetrical relationship not only between kin, where obligations and help were given and received, but also as the principle governing the exchanges of bracelets and necklaces within the *kula*-ring that he borrowed from Malinowski's research. A second principle was the autarkic production and consumption within an economic unit described as householding. On a community level, there was a third type of economic behaviour, described as redistribution. These are contributions given to the chief for storage and future use in community activities such as feasts, trade with other islanders and ceremonial gifts. Reciprocity is an all-encompassing phenomenon but exclusive to tribal societies. Polanyi notes that all social obligations in tribal societies are reciprocal, and fulfilling them serves the individuals give-and-take interest best (Polanyi 2001 [1994]: 48).

Polanyi's three concepts are both descriptive and evaluative, having a moral content. In today's modern society we can associate many exchanges with the three exchange principles, although they appear more blurred, as hazy contours in exchanges mostly governed by monetary market principles but where the state also takes its share. Hardly any transaction within a modern welfare state takes place without the state getting a share of it. From citizens to state, redistribution takes place in the forms of income tax, VAT, pensions, employers' social fees and taxes on gains from capital, inheritance, house sales and so on. The state redistributes these earnings mainly as infrastructure and discounted services, but also directly to households through child allowances, pensions, education benefits, housing subsidies and so on. Redistribution in a modern welfare state such as Sweden is an undisputed fact, not contested and taken for granted by most citizens. It is the amount and encompassment of the redistribution which is contested, expressed in contemporary political ideologies.

Taxation was briefly mentioned in *The Great Transformation* in a very few places. Polanyi saw it as a kind of redistribution because taxation always takes place via the ruler; taxes are paid to the ruler, and the way s/he spends it and redistributes taxes is a political act. Reciprocity thus did not govern taxation. Although Polanyi firmly places taxation under the umbrella of redistribution, we are interested in taxpayers' views on their own contribution vis-à-vis other taxpayers as well as what they receive in return—reciprocity. It is not redistribution that is in focus here; it is the relations created by the very fact of paying taxes.

5. There are currently four main types of Swedish taxes and the Agency is responsible for administrating and collecting all of them. Income tax provides the main funding for municipalities and provinces and makes up about two-thirds of the total tax collected. Income tax is basically applied to all types of personal income including work, pensions and sickness benefits and includes indirect tax on work in the form of social fees. This latter tax is typically paid by the employer on behalf of the employee and does not show in tax returns. The actual tax percentage on income is thus far larger than what is shown on individual tax statements. Second, there is VAT (value added tax—moms), which is included in all consumption prices for private individuals. It is a governmental tax and amounts to almost 20 per cent of total tax collected. The third largest tax comes from capital, mostly on surplus from corporate activity, and amounts to close to 10 per cent. Excise, import and some other small varieties make up the remaining 10 per cent.

6. Quote from Professor Emeritus Sven-Olof Lodin at Skatteakademin, 2015.

7. The result is visualized on the Inglehart–Welzel Cultural Map of the World, showing the vertical axis with 'traditional values' at the lower end escalating towards 'secular–rational values'. On the horizontal axis, 'survival values' are set against 'self-expressional values'. Sweden displays an extreme result on the graph compared with other countries, being situated in the extreme upper right-hand corner.

8. *Fika*, a coffee break, is a common occasion for socializing in Swedish society, at home or in the workplace when taking regular breaks over a cup of coffee or tea, sometimes accompanied by sweet breads or cakes. As a verb you can also *fika*, have a coffee break, with friends. At almost all interviews, I had *fika* with the informants.

9. The tax reform was seen as one of the most radical reforms in any industrialized country in the postwar period (Agell et al. 1996; Steinmo 2002: 840).

10. So-called ordinary people without secondary education in Naples.

11. This of course depends on how you define an exchange. Thinking with Harumi Befu that exchanges can include social ones—agreements, communications, services or other movements between separate units or beings (Befu 1977)—the market appears less dominant.

12. This is perhaps why *The Handbook of Economic Sociology* omits the term, but referring to the work of Max Weber rather speaks about what constitutes an economic relationship.
13. For Bill Maurer, the issue is more methodological. For him, 'the Gift is illuminating a particular notion of the alternative' (2016: xiv). It makes us think that there can be other ways of exchanging, other ways of organizing society. What would '[a]nother law, another economy and another mentality' (ibid.: xiv) make of society?
14. This does not exclude money as a means of exchange. Although Mauss has been interpreted as excluding money from reciprocal relations, for example writing 'that our morality is not solely commercial' (Mauss 2002 [1990]: 63), he also alluded to citizens' relationship with the state and to employers, as he does at the end of *The Gift*; there is necessarily also a concern about money in relation to talking about the state providing social insurance.

LITERATURE

Agell, Jonas, Peter Englund, and Jan Södersten. 1996. Tax Reform of The Century—The Swedish Experiment. *National Tax Journal* 49 (4): 643–664.

Akerlof, George A., and Rachel E. Kranton. 2000. Economics and Identity. *Quarterly Journal of Economics* 115 (3): 715–753. https://doi.org/10.1162/003355300554881

Akerlof, George A., and Robert J. Shiller. 2009. *Animal Spirits: How Human Psychology Drives the Economy, and Why It Matters for Global Capitalism.* Princeton, NJ: Princeton University Press. https://www.google.com/books?hl=sv&lr=&id=2Rz_cuu88DwC&oi=fnd&pg=PR7&dq=animal+spirits+akerlof+shiller+2009&ots=HvzT_P98wA&sig=YJpa64_nQU1RtpoN2fd-CxYNBfQs

Allingham, Michael G., and Agnar Sandmo. 1972. Income Tax Evasion: A Theoretical Analysis. *Journal of Public Economics* 1: 323–338. http://scholar.google.se/scholar?hl=sv&q=sandmo%2C+agnar&btnG=#0

Allvin, Michael. 2004. The Individualization of Labour. In *Learning to Be Employable. New Agendas on Work, Responsibility and Learning in a Globalizing World*, ed. Christina Garsten and Kerstin Jacobsson, 23–41. Basingstoke: Palgrave Macmillan.

Alm, James. 2012. Measuring, Explaining, and Controlling Tax Evasion: Lessons from Theory, Experiments, and Field Studies. *International Tax and Public Finance* 19 (1): 54–77. http://link.springer.com/article/10.1007/s10797-011-9171-2

Alm, James, Roy Bahl, and Matthew N. Murray. 1993. Audit Selection and Income Tax Underreporting in the Tax Compliance Game. *Journal of Development*

Economics 42 (1): 1–33. http://www.sciencedirect.com/science/article/
pii/0304387893900704
Andreoni, James, Brian Erard, and Jonathan Feinstein. 1998. Tax Compliance.
Journal of Economic Literature 36 (2): 818–860. http://www.jstor.org/
stable/2565123
Arkhede, Sofia, and Sören Holmberg. 2015. *Svenska folkets bedömning av offent-
liga myndigheters verksamhet* (Report 19). Göteborg: SOM institutet.
Barnard, A., and J. Spencer. 1996. *Encyclopedia of Social and Cultural Anthropology.*
London and New York: Routledge. https://www.google.com/books?hl=sv&lr=
&id=ReZAlcV7TckC&oi=fnd&pg=PR9&dq=Encyclopedia+of+Social+and+Cul
tural+Anthropology&ots=hZZz7gkBIK&sig=j_tJenBlaItFxPo4TyUY2G-0Yz8
Bazart, C., and A. Bonein. 2014. Reciprocal Relationships in Tax Compliance
Decisions. *Journal of Economic Psychology* 40: 83–102. https://doi.org/10.1016/j.
joep.2012.10.002
Befu, Harumi. 1977. Social Exchange. *Annual Reviews in Anthropology* 6 (1):
255–281.
Bennich-Björkman, Li. 2008. Medborgarsamhället. politisk kultur och politiskt
beteende i Sverige. In *Mellan folkhem och Europa*, ed. Li Bennich-Björkman
and Paula Blomqvist, 40–62. Liber.
Berggren, Henrik, and Lars Trägårdh. 2006. *Är svensken människa? Gemenskap
och oberoende i det moderna Sverige.* Stockholm: Nordstedt.
Björklund Larsen, Lotta. 2010. *Illegal yet Licit: Justifying Informal Purchases of
Work in Contemporary Sweden.* ACTA UNIVE. Stockholm: Stockholm Studies
in Social Anthropology N.S. 2. http://su.diva-portal.org/smash/record.
jsf?pid=diva2:287414
———. 2013. The Making of a 'Good Deal' Dealing with Conflicting and
Complementary Values When Getting the Car Repaired Informally in Sweden.
Journal of Cultural Economy 6: 419–433. http://www.tandfonline.com/doi/
abs/10.1080/17530350.2013.827989
———. 2016. SWEDEN: Failure of a Cooperative Compliance Project? *FairTax
Working Paper No 7.* Umeå.
———. 2017. *Shaping Taxpayers. Values in Action at the Swedish Tax Agency.*
Oxford: Berghahn Books.
Boll, Karen. 2011. *Taxing Assemblages. Laborious and Meticulous Achievements of
Tax Compliance.* Copenhagen: IT University of Copenhagen.
———. 2014a. Mapping Tax Compliance. *Critical Perspectives on Accounting*
25 (4–5): 293–303. http://www.sciencedirect.com/science/article/pii/
S1045235413000270
———. 2014b. Shady Car Dealings and Taxing Work Practices: An Ethnography
of a Tax Audit Process. *Accounting, Organizations and Society* 39 (1): 1–19.
http://www.sciencedirect.com/science/article/pii/S0361368213001001

Bordignon, Massimo. 1993. A Fairness Approach to Income Tax Evasion. *Journal of Public Economics* 52 (3): 345–362. http://www.sciencedirect.com/science/article/pii/004727279390039V

Callon, Michel, and Bruno Latour. 1997. 'Tu Ne Calculeras Pas!' Ou Comment Symétriser Le. In *Le Capitalisme Aujourd'hui*, ed. Alain Caillé, 45–70. Decouverte. http://www.bruno-latour.fr/sites/default/files/P-71-CAPITALISME-MAUSS-FR.pdf

Campbell, John L. 1993. The State and Fiscal Sociology. *Annual Review of Sociology* 19: 163–185. http://www.jstor.org/stable/10.2307/2083385

Cowell, Frank. 1990. *Cheating the Government: The Economics of Evasion*. Cambridge, MA: MIT Press.

Cuco, I., and J. Giner. 2000. Proximal Paradox: Friends and Relatives in the Era of Globalization. *European Journal of Social Theory* 3 (3): 313–324.

Daun, Åke. 2005. *En stuga på sjätte våningen: svensk mentalitet i en mångkulturell värld*. Eslöv: Brutus Östlings Bokförlag. https://scholar.google.se/scholar?hl=sv&q=En+stuga+på+sjätte+våningen%3A+Svensk+mentalitet+i+en+mångkulturell+värld&btnG=

Davies, Charlotte Aull. 1999. *Reflexive Ethnography. A Guide to Researching Selves and Others*. London: Routledge.

Davis, John. 1992. *Exchange*. Minneapolis: University of Minnesota Press.

De Rosa, Pierluigi. 2014. Building Trust in Italian Tax Authority. An Ethnographic Approach. *Rivista Internazionale di Scienze Sociali* 124 (1): 103–130.

de Swaan, Abram. 1988. *In Care of the State: Health Care, Education and Welfare in Europe and the USA in the Modern Era*. Cambridge: Polity Press.

de Waal, F.B.M. 2000. Attitudinal Reciprocity in Food Sharing among Brown Capuchin Monkeys. *Animal Behaviour* 60: 253–261. http://www.sciencedirect.com/science/article/pii/S0003347200914714

Derrida, Jacques. 1995. *The Gift of Death*. Vol. 25. Chicago: University of Chicago Press.

Engström, Per, and Bertil Holmlund. 2006. Tax Evasion and Self-Employment in a High-Tax Country: Evidence from Sweden. *CESIFO Working Paper No. 1736*.

Fehr, Ernst, and Armin Falk. 2002. Psychological Foundations of Incentives. *European Economic Review* 46 (4–5): 687–724. http://www.sciencedirect.com/science/article/pii/S0014292101002082

Feldman, Naomi E., and Joel Slemrod. 2009. War and Taxation: When Does Patriotism Overcome the Free-Rider Impulse. In *The New Fiscal Sociology: Taxation in Comparative and Historical Perspective*, ed. Isaac William Martin, Ajay K. Mehrotra, and Monica Prasad, 138–154. Cambridge: Cambridge University Press. https://www.google.com/books?hl=sv&lr=&id=vdzgZwhuFZUC&oi=fnd&pg=PA138&dq=Feldman+%26+Slemrod&ots=IkrDERlxsJ&sig=MZBjiUfEO42SyBGY0069hk1IaFc

Firth, Raymond. 1959. *Social Change in Tikopia*. London and New York: George Allen & Unwin.

Fortin, Bernard, Guy Lacroix, and Marie-Claire Villeval. 2007. Tax Evasion and Social Interactions. *Journal of Public Economics* 91 (11–12): 2089–2012. http://www.sciencedirect.com/science/article/pii/S0047272707000497

Frey, Bruno S., and Benno Torgler. 2007. Tax Morale and Conditional Cooperation. *Journal of Comparative Economics* 35: 136–159. http://www.sciencedirect.com/science/article/pii/S0147596706000849

Frykman, Jonas, and Kjell Hansen. 2009. Welfare State, Health and Local Culture. http://tryggvar.se/publikationer/welfare_state_health_and_local_culture.pdf

Gavanas, Anna, and Catarina Calleman. 2013. *Rena Hem På Smutsiga Villkor?: Hushållstjänster, Migration Och Globalisering*. Göteborg: Makadam förlag.

Geertz, Clifford. 1973. *The Interpretation of Cultures*. New York: Basic Books.

Godbout, Jacques, and Alain Caille. 1998. *The World of the Gift*. Montreal: McGill-Queen's University Press.

Gordon, James P.F. 1989. Individual Morality and Reputation Costs as Deterrents to Tax Evasion. *European Economic Review* 33: 797–805. http://www.sciencedirect.com/science/article/pii/0014292189900263

Gracia, Louise, and Lynne Oats. 2012. Boundary Work and Tax Regulation: A Bourdieusian View. *Accounting, Organizations and Society* 37 (5): 304–321. https://doi.org/10.1016/j.aos.2012.03.004

Graeber, David. 2001. *Toward an Anthropological Theory of Value: The False Coin of Our Own Dreams*. New York: Palgrave Macmillan.

Graham, Mark. 2002. Emotional Bureaucracies: Emotions Civil Servants, and Immigrants in the Swedish Welfare State. *Ethos* 30 (3): 199–226. https://doi.org/10.1525/eth.2002.30.3.199

Gregory, C.A. 1994. Exchange and Reciprocity. *Companion Encyclopaedia of Anthropology*: 911–939.

Gribnau, H. 2013. Legal Certainty: A Matter of Principle. In *Retroactivity of Tax Legislation*, ed. Hans Gribnau and Melvin Pauwels, 69–95. Amsterdam: EATLP.

Gribnau, Hans. 2015. Taxation, Reciprocity and Communicative Regulation. *Tilburg Law Review* 20: 191–212. http://booksandjournals.brillonline.com/content/journals/10.1163/22112596-02002009

Guala, Francesco. 2012. Reciprocity: Weak or Strong? What Punishment Experiments Do (and Do Not) Demonstrate. *Behavioral and Brain Sciences* 35 (1): 1–15. https://doi.org/10.1017/S0140525X11000069

Gudeman, Stephen. 2001. *The Anthropology of Economy: Community, Market, and Culture*. Oxford: Blackwell Publishers.

Hadenius, Axel. 1985. Citizens Strike a Balance: Discontent with Taxes, Content with Spending. *Journal of Public Policy* 5 (3): 349–363. http://journals.cambridge.org/abstract_S0143814X00003159

Hanousek, J., and F. Palda. 2004. Quality of Government Services and the Civic Duty to Pay Taxes in the Czech and Slovak Republics, and Other Transition Countries. *Kyklos* 57 (2): 237–252. http://onlinelibrary.wiley.com/doi/10.1111/j.0023-5962.2004.00252.x/full

Hansson, Ingemar. 2011. Företagets inställning till skatter är en styrelsefråga. *Dagens Industri* 18 (5): 2011.

Hart, Keith. 2007. Marcel Mauss: In Pursuit of the Whole. A Review Essay. *Comparative Studies in Society and History* 49 (2): 473–485.

Herrmann, Gretchen M. 1997. Gift or Commodity: What Changes Hands in the US Garage Sale? *American Ethnologist* 24 (4): 910–930.

High, Holly, and Clare Hall. 2012. Re-Reading the Potlatch in a Time of Crisis: Debt and the Distinctions That Matter 1. *Social Anthropology* 20 (4): 363–379. https://doi.org/10.1111/j.1469-8676.2012.00218.x

Holmberg, Sören, and Nora Oleskog Tryggvason. 2014. *Svenska folkets bedömning av offentliga myndigheters verksamhet* (Report 11). Göteborg: SOM-institutet.

Inglehart, Ronald. 2006. Inglehart-Welzel Cultural Map of the World. *World Values Survey*. https://scholar.google.se/scholar?q=Inglehart-Welzel+Cultural+Map+of+the+World&btnG=&hl=sv&as_sdt=0%2C5

Jacobsson, Kerstin. 2006. *Durkheims moralsociologi och välfärdsstaten*. http://www.score.su.se/polopoly_fs/1.26584.1320939799!/20063.pdf

Kirchler, Erich. 2007. *The Economic Psychology of Tax Behaviour*. Cambridge: Cambridge University Press. https://www.google.com/books?hl=sv&lr=&id=dh0qhqTOtb0C&oi=fnd&pg=PR7&dq=erich+kirchler&ots=no1ZAAWlKd&sig=HsX_aai3HBSgF0_xX4cKtKoULIM

Komter, Aafke E. 1996. *The Gift: An Interdisciplinary Perspective*. Amsterdam: Amsterdam University Press. https://www.google.com/books?hl=sv&lr=&id=o7wq4oO2B0YC&oi=fnd&pg=PA1&dq=the+gift+komter+1996&ots=rr0d8yW9pn&sig=rF8xKWNVD5BJSJtl11bf0YgUGLQ

———. 2014. Idealized Versus Real-Life Reciprocity: How to Strike the Balance? *Netherlands Journal of Legal Philosophy* 43 (2): 158–171.

Kornhauser, Marjorie E. 2007. Tax Morale Approach to Compliance: Recommendations for the IRS, A. *Florida Tax Review* 8 (6): 599–634. http://heinonlinebackup.com/hol-cgi-bin/get_pdf.cgi?handle=hein.journals/ftaxr8&section=27

L'Estoile, Benoit De. 2014. 'Money Is Good, but a Friend Is Better'. Uncertainty, Orientation to the Future and 'The Economy'. *Current Anthropology* 55 (S9): 62–73. http://halshs.archives-ouvertes.fr/hal-00935026/

Ledeneva, A.V. 1998. *Russia's Economy of Favours: Blat, Networking, and Informal Exchange*. Cambridge: Cambridge University Press.

Lévi-Strauss, Claude. 1966. *The Savage Mind*. Chicago: University of Chicago Press. http://www.citeulike.org/group/716/article/197326

Lewin, Leif. 2008. Samling Kring Folkhemmet. In *Mellan Folkhem Och Europa*, ed. Li Bennich-Björkman and Paula Blomqvist, 20–39. Liber.

Lindbeck, Assar, Sten Nyberg, and Jörgen W. Weibull. 1999. Social Norms and Economic Incentives in the Welfare State. *Quarterly Journal of Economics* CXIV (1): 1–35. http://www.jstor.org/stable/2586946

Lodin, Sven-Olof. 2007. Några Kvalitetskrav På En God Skattelagstiftning. *Skattenytt* 2007 (9): 477–490.

MacCormack, Geoffrey. 1976. Reciprocity. *Man* 11 (1): 89–103. http://www.jstor.org/stable/2800390

Malinowski, Bronislaw. 1966 [1922]. Argonauts of the Western Pacific. London: Routledge & Kegan Paul. https://scholar.google.se/scholar?hl=sv&q=malino wski+1922&btnG=#5

Martin, Isaac William, Ajay K. Mehrotra, and Monica Prasad. 2009. *The New Fiscal Sociology: Taxation in Comparative and Historical Perspective.* Cambridge: Cambridge University Press. http://www.cambridge.org/gb/knowledge/ isbn/item2427351/?site_locale=en_GB

Maurer, Bill. 2016. Foreword: Puzzles and Pathways. In *The Gift: Expanded Edition/Marcel Mauss.* Selected, Annotated and Translated by Jane I. Guyer, ix–xvii. Chicago: HAU Books.

Mauss, Marcel. 2002 [1990]. *The Gift.* London: Routledge.

———. 2016. *The Gift: Expanded Edition/Marcel Mauss.* Selected, Annotated and Translated by Jane I. Guyer. Chicago: Hau Books.

Mulligan, Emer, and Lynne Oats. 2015. Tax Professionals at Work in Silicon Valley. *Accounting, Organizations and Society* 52: 63–76.

Musgrave, R.A. 1992. Schumpeter's Crisis of the Tax State: An Essay in Fiscal Sociology. *Journal of Evolutionary Economics* 2 (2): 89–113. https://doi. org/10.1007/BF01193535

Narotzky, Susana, and Paz Moreno. 2002. Reciprocity's Dark Side: Negative Reciprocity, Morality and Social Reproduction. *Anthropological Theory* 2 (3): 281–305.

Oats, Lynne, and Diana Onu. 2016. Tax Talk: An Exploration of Online Discussions Among Taxpayers. *Journal of Business Ethics*: 1–14. https://doi. org/10.1007/s10551-016-3032-y

Offer, Avner. 1997. Between the Gift and the Market: The Economy of Regard. *The Economic History Review* 50 (3): 450–476.

Ortner, Sheryl B. 2003. *New Jersey Dreaming: Capital, Culture, and the Class of '58.* Durham, NC: Duke University Press.

Pardo, Italo. 1996. *Managing Existence in Naples: Morality, Action, and Structure.* Cambridge: Cambridge University Press.

Polanyi, Karl. 2001 [1944]. *The Great Transformation: The Political and Economic Origins of Our Time.* Boston: Beacon Press. https://scholar.google.se/scholar ?hl=sv&q=polanyi&btnG=#1

Pommerehne, Werner W., Albert Hart, and Bruno S. Frey. 1994. Tax Morale, Tax Evasion and the Choice of Policy Instruments in Different Political Systems.

Public Finance 49 (Supplement): 52–69. https://ideas.repec.org/a/pfi/pub-fin/v49y1994isupplementp52-69.html

Portes, Alejandro, Manuel Castells, and Lauren A. Benton. 1989. *The Informal Economy: Studies in Advanced and Less Developed Countries.* Baltimore, MD: Johns Hopkins University Press.

Rabin, Matthew. 1998. Psychology and Economics. *Journal of Economic Literature* 36: 11–46. http://www.jstor.org/stable/2564950

Rawlings, Gregory, and Valerie Braithwaite. 2003. Voices for Change: Australian Perspectives on Tax Administration. *Australian Journal of Social Issues (Australian Council of Social Service)* 38 (3): 263–268.

Rosenberg, Göran. 2013. Sweden: The Reluctant Nation. In *Populist Fantasies: European Revolts in Context,* ed. Catherine Fieschi, Marley Morris, and Lila Caballero, 151–209. Counterpoint. http://counterpoint.uk.com/wp-content/uploads/2013/10/Populist-Fantasies-European-revolts-in-context.pdf#page=82

Rothstein, Bo. 1992. *Den Korporativa Staten: Intresseorganisationer Och Statsförvaltning I Svensk Politik.* Stockholm: Norstedts.

Sahlins, Marshall D. 1972. *Stone Age Economics.* London: Routledge.

San Juan, Eric A. 2013. Cultural Jurisprudence. *Asian Pacific Law & Policy Journal* 15 (1). https://litigation-essentials.lexisnexis.com/webcd/app?action=DocumentDisplay&crawlid=1&doctype=cite&docid=15+Asian-Pacific+L.+%26+Pol'y+J.+1&srctype=smi&srcid=3B15&key=6d4241831616c4765b24e20143f893b0

Schneider, Friedrich, and Dominik H. Enste. 2002. *The Shadow Economy: An International Survey.* Cambridge: Cambridge University Press. http://www.google.com/books?hl=sv&lr=&id=tMzmHgd2qNcC&oi=fnd&pg=PR7&ots=sEf4vbyyTM&sig=bDIlmRotakrfnLn30AAUtPUwmWE

Schnellenbach, Jan. 2010. Vertical and Horizontal Reciprocity in a Theory of Taxpayer Compliance. In *Developing Alternative Frameworks for Explaining Tax Compliance,* ed. James Alm, Juan Martinez-Vasquez, and Benno Torgler, 56–73. New York, NY: Routledge International Studies in Money and Banking.

Schumpeter, Joseph A. 1954. The Crisis of the Tax State. *International Economic Papers* 4: 5–38.

Skatteverket. 2007. *Svartköp och svartjobb i Sverige. Del 2: Möjliga åtgärder mot svartarbete och bidragsfusk.* Solna: Skatteverket.

———. 2008. *Mätning av skatteverkets effekter på dess omgivning.* Solna: Skatteverket.

———. 2012. *Medborgarnas synpunkter på skattesystemet, skattefusket och Skatteverkets kontroll.* Solna: Skatteverket.

———. 2014. *Verksamhetsplan för Skatteverket.* Solna: Skatteverket.

Slater, Don. 2002. From Calculation to Alienation: Disentangling Economic Abstractions. *Economy and Society* 31 (2): 234. Routledge. http://search.ebscohost.com/login.aspx?direct=true&db=bth&AN=6446266&site=ehost-live

Slemrod, Joel B. 1992. *Why People Pay Taxes: Tax Compliance and Enforcement.* Edited by Joel B. Slemrod. Ann Arbor: University of Michigan Press.

———. 2007. Cheating Ourselves: The Economics of Tax Evasion. *The Journal of Economic Perspectives* 21 (1): 25–48. http://www.jstor.org/stable/30033700

Smith, K.W. 1992. Reciprocity and Fairness: Positive Incentives for Tax Compliance. In *Why People Pay Taxes, Tax Compliance and Enforcement*, ed. Joel B. Slemrod, 223–250. Ann Arbor: University of Michigan Press.

Spicer, Michael W., and S.B. Lundstedt. 1976. Understanding Tax Evasion. *Public Finance* 30 (4). https://works.bepress.com/michael_spicer/?paginate=1&page=4&page_size=25

Steinmo, Sven. 1996. *Taxation and Democracy: Swedish, British, and American Approaches to Financing the Modern State*. Yale University Press.

Steinmo, S. 2002. Globalization and Taxation Challenges to the Swedish Welfare State. *Comparative Political Studies* 35 (7): 839–862. http://cps.sagepub.com/content/35/7/839.short

Stridh, Anders, and Lennart Wittberg. 2015. *Från Fruktad Skattefogde till Omtyckt Servicemyndighet*. Solna: Skatteverket.

Svallfors, Stefan. 1995. The End of Class Politics? Structural Cleavages and Attitudes to Swedish Welfare Policies. *Acta Sociologica* 38 (1): 53–74.

Swedberg, Richard. 2003. *Principles of Economic Sociology*. Princeton, NJ: Princeton University Press.

Thomassen, Bjorn. 2015. Begging Rome: Norms at the Margins, Norms of the in-Between. *Critique of Anthropology*. http://coa.sagepub.com/content/35/1/94.short

Westerman, Pauline. 2014. Reciprocity: A Fragile Equilibrium. *Netherlands Journal of Legal Philosophy* 2 (43): 172–184.

Widlok, Thomas. 2013. Allowing Others to Take What is Valued. *HAU: Journal of Ethnographic Theory* 3 (2): 11–31.

Williams, Colin C., and Jan Windebank. 1998. *Informal Employment in the Advanced Economies: Implications for Work and Welfare*. London: Routledge.

CHAPTER 2

Taxpayers' Relation to Their State

Abstract This chapter deals with taxation as a reciprocal relationship between taxpayers and the state they live in. Taxpayers are often seen to evaluate their benefits relative to the tax burden; whether the tax paid accords with what they perceive they are receiving in return. Such a view embraces a broader, reciprocal view of taxes paid and welfare benefits received. Focus is on taxpayers' perceptions of contributing with taxes, or receiving from the common treasure chest, and what this has to do with seeing taxation as part of a reciprocal relation. This chapter looks into such aspects of taxation from the citizens' perspective and also observes how the Agency thinks about those from whom they collect taxes; from paying tribute to customer.

Keywords Justifying tax avoidance • Fair taxation • Taxation as a system of total prestations • Tit-for-tat reciprocity • Equality reciprocity

'I tell you why I buy work off the books. This family has paid far too much to the state already', complained Henry, a former neighbour. It was a crisp autumn day and we were raking leaves on each side of our fence. Taking a break and chitchatting over the fence, we spoke about work. Henry had a well-paid job as an administrator at a bank and his wife Gunilla worked as a teacher. They had recently refurbished part of their house, designed the extension themselves but had had craftsmen in to do the work. Obviously, following Henry's cue, some if not all of the recompense to the craftsmen had been made *svart*.

© The Author(s) 2018   49
L. Björklund Larsen, *A Fair Share of Tax*,
https://doi.org/10.1007/978-3-319-69772-7_2

Taxpayers are often seen to evaluate their benefits relative to the tax burden (Folger 1986); whether the tax paid accords with what they perceive they are receiving in return (cf. Cowell 1990; Falkinger 1995). Such a view embraces a broader, reciprocal view of taxes paid and welfare benefits received. Compliance can from this perspective be described as a tit-for-tat relation (cf. Björklund Larsen 2010) and something that a tax collecting agency has difficulty in making an impact on, unless it is seen as corrupt with its officials lining their own pockets (Aidt 2003).

Justifying tax cheating seems a common practice. Swedes can also find similar reasoning and excuses that justify tax cheating as a result of their state's lack of fiscal fairness and universalist spending on the one hand and the same state's 'seemingly capricious application of rights, duties and entitlements' on the other, as Italians do (Guano 2010: 488; cf. Pardo 1996). Tax compliance has reciprocal ingredients and the act of collecting taxes is closely connected, yet not exclusive, to their redistribution. It matters how taxes are spent in relation to our perceived payment.

If citizens believe that the government acts—spends—in their own interest, that government procedures are fair and that their trust in both the state and other citizens will be reciprocated, then their propensity to pay taxes is considerably higher, even though it might not be in their short-term interest to do so (Kornhauser 2007).

In this chapter we will look into such aspects of taxation from the citizens' perspective and from how the Agency thinks about those from whom they collect taxes. We will briefly engage with the history of Swedish tax revenue collection, how they have talked about the taxpayer and move on to spend most of the discussion on today's strategies. As we are interested in the Agency's relation to taxpayers we will see how its employees regard, communicate with and treat taxpayers in their aim to increase compliance. Then we turn to the *Limningers*. How do they see their relationship with the state? Seeing taxation as creating reciprocity provides ample possibilities for justifying their engagement with *svart arbete* in various ways.

TAXES IN TERMS OF RECIPROCITY CANNOT BE MEASURED

Henry's family had paid far too much to the state, he said. Such a claim can never be substantiated, as obviously we can never measure the extent of tax transfers. These are perceptions: although a citizen knows how much tax s/he pays through the annual statement there are also VAT, social fees and other indirect taxes which are added to more or less every economic transaction taking place in Sweden. Although we can add up how much direct tax we pay, indirect taxes are difficult to account for as they are not always clearly stated. On the receipt side there is obviously no way to estimate the pay-off—how much welfare and other governmental services are given in return (for taxes paid). Exchanges, for example tax payments, between inhabitants and state are vast even on a daily basis, and are impossible to quantify or account for, and immensely complicated in a welfare state.

Recognizing reciprocity, the receive side is as important to consider, as we also want to evaluate what we get for taxes paid. What is the worth of my daily welfare services? How can I evaluate the standard of the streets I walk? What is the value of the health services I receive in times of need? What is the worth of the schooling I have attended, or that my children have gone through? Is the state I pay tax to governed by values I share? In quantitative terms these are silly questions, but from a qualitative perspective they are important, as various nations have defined their services—such as the welfare they provide—differently. Such calculative endeavour is completely futile. What we get for taxes paid is rather a comparison in time and space; of a glorified past where things were rosier and the state more generous or giving services of better quality. It could also be the opposite, where we recognize improvement over how things were in the past. The same comparison goes for space—comparing what we get with that which other municipalities/regions/nations provide for their members.

Yet, as we will see, in Sweden there is a recognition of a such a reciprocal relationship. From a resident's perspective, taxes paid do indeed have an impact on the expectations of what society should provide. To underline, it is a perception game. This is also why reciprocity is a better way to express the relation between states and their citizens instead of through an expected monetary outcome of a series of taxable market exchanges.

Such a change of focus moves our scrutiny away from tax percentages as an explanatory factor for the propensity of citizens to pay their taxes (cf. Allingham and Sandmo 1972). A very simplified conclusion of Allingham and Sandmo's article is that taxpayers are always maximizing their income in relation to tax payment and penalty fees. Accordingly, a taxpayer will report and pay just enough tax, weighing the outcome of successful tax avoidance against being caught and paying penalties. It is not only at the Swedish Agency that this seminal model has been used to create strategies against evasion in order to increase compliance (Skatteverket 2005). As we saw in Chap. 1, there are many, many issues other than economic benefits that make taxpayers pay up, and this is something the Agency acknowledges (Skatteverket 2010). The willingness to pay tax reflects many aspects about what it is to be a citizen.

But, as we will see in what follows, there is still a large element of economic reasoning among Swedes. The point is to move focus from actual monetary amounts to reasoning about what such money is spent on; we will change the scrutiny from quantitative to qualitative views of expenditure.

THE AGENCY'S VIEW ON WHY TAXPAYERS COMPLY

The earliest notions of Swedish tax collection occurred during the thirteenth century (Odén 1967: 3). The aim was, as elsewhere, to finance the king's army and the warfare it undertook. Although some cash could be collected, most tax was paid in kind. Taxes could be butter, oxen, grain, fish and hides, and it was not until 1869 that taxes had to be paid in money.

It was early on understood that these taxes were insufficient and whoever was in power introduced new taxes and fees in order to increase government revenue. Already from the middle ages there was a difference between annual taxes on the one hand and taxes extracted as and when needed on the other. This is a difference that continued until modern times (Borg 2008). Tolls and customs excises were introduced over the centuries, and taxes were extracted on the consumption of luxury goods, such as the tax on glass windows (Löwnertz 1983). Introduced in 1743, such taxes were smart and efficient, as glass windows could not be hidden. The state was already paying attention to fairness: as it was recognized that income differed between regions, so did taxes on glass windows—with Stockholm, the capital, having a higher rate than the countryside. Other taxes and tolls were added through the years; the list is very long (see Björklund Larsen 2017: 10), and it provides an interesting insight into both old Sweden and the many ingenious ideas about extracting income almost exclusively from the poor, Sweden providing just one example of this. Needless to say, the poor did not always appreciate this fiscal attention.

If people did not agree with paying their dues, they probably did not have much of a choice except by hiding what ought to have been subject to tax. This was not so easy. In sixteenth-century Sweden the king owned the land and what belonged to the homestead owners was what grew in the soil. Taxes were therefore seen as rent from the land; it was a ground tax (Ekman 2003a) that the king could justify as being fair: it was his land after all. For centuries annual taxes were based upon property and made possible by kings keeping track of people's ownership of land. Although the control, collection, organization and levels of this ground tax changed throughout the centuries, it remained in use until the beginning of the twentieth century (Löwnertz 2003). This probes the question that tax is something more than that defined in the *Swedish National Encyclopaedia* as, '[T]ax is a statutory payment to the public without direct reciprocity' (www.ne.se, accessed 16.2.2017). There has been a history of legitimizing at least certain taxes by getting something back for the payment. Swedish taxpayers have expected to get something for what they have contributed to the state.[1]

Joseph Schumpeter claimed that in order to understand any society and its political life, one of the best starting points is taxation (1954). The development of the tax system—laws and the organization of tax collection—can therefore be seen as a sign of its time that reflects the views of society (Björklund Larsen 2017: 57). Bailiffs in the early times of Swedish taxation history were seen as harsh, and they extorted taxes from locals (Magnus 1976 [1555, 1909]). This is in sharp contrast to the contemporary efficient and service-minded Agency employee who is supposed to treat taxpayers with respect, making it easy to do right and difficult to err (Skatteverket 2014). A tax system that evolves from one that is seen as extortion to one affecting social and cultural values in order to make people comply voluntarily means that both lawmakers and tax authorities in particular pay attention to that their actions are legitimate.

FAIRNESS IN TAX COLLECTION

The contemporary Agency has been apt to follow research on compliance that says the less the taxpayer deals with his own tax statements and payments the more correct taxes become. The Agency has very successfully implemented one of its mottos: 'it should be easy to do right and difficult to err' (Skatteverket 2013: 20, my translation).[2] Research on taxation has shown that to increase compliance one should minimize taxpayers' manual entries on tax return forms (e.g. Daunton 2001). Income tax is basically applied to all types of personal income, including work, pensions and sickness benefits, and includes indirect tax on work in the form of social fees. These taxes are typically paid by the employer on behalf of the employee. Contemporary income tax reporting is for most Swedes a very simple task and to a high degree a computerized process. The yearly tax return for employees is highly automated and filing is usually very simple. Salaries are directly transferred into employee bank accounts as net income, and employers pay the deducted tax amounts monthly to the Agency. Employers provide a standardized form—a control income statement— early in the year for all employees.

In early spring a prepopulated tax return form is delivered to all those who have had income reported, either as employees or as self-employed. The form states income, taxed fringe benefits and other related information for the previous income year. There is therefore seldom any manual reporting to do; figures for wages and income tax deducted are provided by the employer, and mortgage institutions and banks report interest received and paid; even information about subsidized service deductions such as RUT and ROT are preprinted—and the various taxes paid, of course. The great majority of individuals are only required to confirm this information electronically—by telephone, text message, an app or on the Agency's website. There is obviously the opportunity to add income or deductions, but most employed Swedes just authorize the information once they have checked the figures on the prefilled tax return and simply accept it with an electronic signature, in some cases after making a few changes. The Agency encourages citizens to confirm their annual tax returns electronically by promising that any tax repayments from such returns will occur just in time for the summer vacation. The annual tax return is quite simple, the appearance of equal treatment is underscored and all employees seem to be treated in the same way. The result is that most employed people do not have much of a choice except to pay taxes that are due.

I have not been able to find contemporary estimates of how much time a Swedish taxpayer spends on average on their tax return, but it is definitely much, much less than the American average of twenty-seven hours (Lepore 2012). After the centennial tax reform of 1991, the average time spent was significantly reduced from two hours and twenty-one minutes in 1992 to one hour and forty-two minutes the following year. There is no reason to think that it has increased, but rather the opposite. Self-employed citizens and other commercial entities have more cumbersome tax return procedures, however. The Agency pays more attention to the self-employed, as errors on such tax returns seem to proliferate compared to those of the employed citizens (Skatteverket 2013). Continuous digitalization, automation and technological improvements apart, there is also quite general acceptance of the redistribution of fiscal revenue. Swedes pay a lot in taxes but as long as they get good services for these payments they will continue to pay up.

If the percentage you pay plays a role in willingness to comply, one additional reason why Swedes comply is that is quite difficult to see how much income tax an individual in reality pays. For example, social fees do not show up in individual tax returns as they are paid directly by employers and are considered outside the scope of income tax. The actual tax percentage as fiscal revenue to the state on personal income is thus far larger than what is shown on individual tax statements. Swedes hear about the high tax levels paid by international comparison, yet looking at their own tax statements, the percentage appears to be a lot smaller.

Who Is the Taxpayer?

Looking at the Agency mottos over the years acknowledges their attention to tax compliance's reciprocal element. In what was probably the very first information campaign, in 1955, the Swedish finance department ran a number of slogans addressing citizens and emphasizing that taxes financed welfare: *Skatterna bär upp försvaret* (taxes support defence); *Våra skolor danar framtidens Sverige* (our schools fashion Sweden's future); *Att bli sjuk utan att bli ruinerad* (being sick without going bankrupt); and *Att få åldras utan oro* (to age without anxiety) (Thärnström 2003: 119). The core tasks of a welfare state are to finance defence, education, health and pensions, and the finance department's implicit message was that Swedish citizens ought to contribute if they were going to have some of these wonders in return. This still applies. As one of the Agency's analysts said:

> [T]he logical conclusion is that citizens are willing to pay more tax if s/he can trust that all others (taxpayers) provide more and that s/he can trust that the political institutions provide us with better services in return. It is thus about reciprocity—to feel that you get something in return for the sacrifice of paying tax. And the opposite is of course also possible; if the tax avoidance increases we have a vicious circle.

Individuals and other taxpayers (corporations, organizations, etc.) will be less willing to pay their tax if compatriots cheat. If fiscal income decreases, there is less revenue to spend on good quality public services. The perceived value of services given for the tax paid is reduced and the willingness to comply with taxes decreases even more (Skatteverket 2010: 12).

The finance department has given the task of working with tax compliance to the Agency. The transformation of the Agency can be illustrated by changed strategies, its depiction of taxpayers and its mottos over the years. This has not come easy. The Agency has during the last fifty years worked hard and explicitly to increase compliance, adapting its collecting services and the control of reported and actual tax income in many ways (Ekman 2003a; Skatteverket 2005; Björklund Larsen 2017). From mere retaliation strategies, the Agency has increasingly circled around the issue of heeding research about (voluntary) tax compliance in their analyses and consequent work in formulating strategies.

Changed communication strategies with those deemed liable to pay recognizes the reciprocal element. For many years Swedish taxpayers were referred to as *skattskyldiga*, tax indebted individuals, at the Agency (Stridh and Wittberg 2015: 23). Its employees even had an abbreviation for all 'tax indebted' people, *sksk*, pronounced as the four letters. Naturally, this impersonalized taxpayers made the distance even greater between Agency employees and the people they ought to serve (ibid.).

A person who is indebted has a completely different status from the one that a payer acquires. As Mauss stated, the gift is a social phenomenon with three obligations; to give, to receive and to reciprocate. An important aspect of exchanges is thus to emphasize who initiates them. This is not just a rhetorical question: one might wonder what would happen to reciprocity and the way it has been analysed if an exchange were to start with the act of taking instead of giving. More emphasis might have been put on the recipient, or rather the taker, as the initiator of an exchange if Mauss had translated the Maori proverb in the right sequence (Narotzky and Moreno 2002).

The Maori account Mauss used is based on a translation in 1855 by a Reverend Taylor, and the giving and taking concerns the doings of Maru, a god of justice and war. However, this translation has been questioned. In a historic analysis of 'organizing' within the Auschwitz extermination camp, Susana Narotzky and Paz Moreno argue that reciprocity as a concept is only useful if seen in the light of moral implications, taking account of both the negative and positive aspects (Narotzky and Moreno 2002: 282). Although a far-fetched contextual comparison, it is one I lean on when claiming that reciprocity as a human feeling is universal (cf. Gouldner 1960). Reciprocity is often linked to social stability, creating community and society through exchanges. The bonds between individuals generate morals, rights and duties between people—'a world of mutual obligation' (Narotzky and Moreno 2002: 285). In their argument there is a tension between the actions of giving and of taking, maybe thanks to a faulty translation of the Maori proverb, as mentioned above (ibid.: 288).

If we reinterpret the proverb, instead of starting with the generous undertaking of giving, the Maori god Maru begins by taking *before* proceeding to give back. This changes the meaning fundamentally, and especially how reciprocity is perceived and acted upon. Having taken something means an obligation to give back, which means that a deliberate action is expected; otherwise the relationship would be immersed in hostility. Having had something taken, or been obligated to give, transforms the 'giver' into one who waits to be reciprocated. If nothing happens and no counterexchange is offered, it may result in a state of passivity where expectations accumulate and the passive needy recipient is increasingly distanced; will s/he ever get anything back? This interesting aspect of reciprocity is 'the articulation between forms of political generosity and the legitimisation of claims over resources and the tension between acceptance and rejection among those contributing to the accumulation of a distribution pool' (Narotzky and Moreno 2002: 286). If we translate this reasoning to the Swedish welfare state, it supports the view that the distributive transfers that have the least support among the population are those that are the least general; those where recipients have to demonstrate their need (Svallfors 1996: 56). They have to claim something to be given back, instead of just receiving it.

When the Agency changes how it addresses citizens by calling them taxpayers, their status improves. A taxpayer is one who has contributed and is now expecting to get something back. Although the Agency does not distribute any revenues, the least it can do as a governmental authority is to treat the payers well; they have the upper hand. The opposite is reasonable if citizens are referred to as offering tribute. Citizens have already received services and welfare; they are indebted, subordinated and minors, and it is their very duty to pay up!

Following governmental administrative fashions, the Agency decided at one point to regard the taxpayer as a customer. This decision took effect during 1991–2 (Malmer 2003: 50), when citizens were told that there was only one point of contact for all their tax issues, a 'one-customer relation' (Ekman 2003b: 80). It was stated that '[w]e are a modern and efficient administration and we work from a processual and customer oriented approach. The citizens and corporations can make use of our service at their leisure' (Johansson 2003: 117, my translation). The emphasis in this depiction of 'taxpayer as customer' was on the quality and approach of the Agency's services. The Agency was there for the citizens, so it should be easy to reach the Agency and to understand the demands of taxation, and the Agency should display its willingness to serve (ibid.: 111).

But is it valid to depict citizens as customers when they have no choice whether or not to use the services on offer (Drewry 2005)? A customer can decide what, where and when to shop, whereas taxpayers have few choices if they want to obey laws, rules and regulations. Seeing a citizen who pays tax (*skattebetalare*—a taxpayer) as a customer provides this individual with certain rights; if nothing else, these rights include being given the correct information and help in paying taxes due. This is the other side of the taxpayer–customer coin; the focus on the reciprocal obligations that are fundamental to citizenship and contractual relationships risks being submerged. Such a view can also have a Janus face. A taxpayer as customer makes for a more direct, market relationship—paying an amount and getting value for it. Although the intention of such an approach was to treat taxpayers better and to be more service minded, the risk is that taxes become more directly seen as a market exchange.

Despite these critical views on the customer metaphor, the Agency's various strategies have largely paid off. At the start of the twenty-first century, the work that had started in the 1970s came into full effect. Since 2006, the Agency has been among the governmental authorities that citizens find most reliable (Ekonomistyrningsverket 2012), a place it continues to have (as shown in *Myndighetsbarometern* 2017). And this is regardless of respondents' political opinions, gender, class or age (Engelbrecht and Holmberg 2012: 9).

A Contemporary View of Taxpayers at the Agency

An efficient Agency with friendly, reliable and amenable employees is seen to be doing its job well, and has created a perception among the Swedish population that everybody else is paying: it is therefore trusted (Björklund Larsen 2017: 72ff). The reasoning goes that if I trust that the Agency is doing its job well for me and my taxes, I will trust that other taxpayers are getting the same treatment. The Agency diligently works at estimating and collecting the right tax while also informing taxpayers of this work. This cannot be achieved by words on a website alone, but has to be enforced in practice by controls and audits as well as communicating details of its work.

Yet it is not only what the Agency does that has an impact on tax compliance among the Swedish population; it is also the behaviour of other bureaucracies. And this is something the Agency recognizes. 'When other bureaucracies in society—those that have the task of spending what the Agency has collected—apply values that resonate with those held by the public, it will, ceteris paribus, automatically increase the Agency's reputation,' said the manager of the analysis department at a presentation about the current standing of the Agency (cf. Björklund Larsen 2017: 178). So the Agency recognizes that the willingness for citizens to pay up depends on whether the revenue collected is well spent and on services that taxpayers find relevant. It is a perceived reciprocity with the government and its institutions, and such behaviour will increase tax compliance.

Recognizing reciprocity as a constituent of what makes for increased tax compliance is important at the Agency. It argues that it is logical to believe that citizens will pay more of their taxes if:

1. The taxpayer can trust that all other taxpayers pay *more*, and
2. That s/he can trust that the political institutions will provide *more* services (Skatteverket 2010: 12).

The second argument was discussed in Chap. 1, where it was seen that reciprocity plays a role in getting benefits for what is paid—a tit-for-tat relationship. Important to note is that taxation is not a market transaction, which would bring an immediacy and a specificity to the resulting relation. It is naive to argue that a citizen wants to see what his/her tax money is spent on and compare what is received in return; there is just no way to calculate what the state provides. But the argument is very common—recall my former neighbour Henry.

Now, in the first statement the Agency not only talks about a status quo of tax collection; the statement is also about *increasing* taxation. The keyword is *more*. Adding more is to my mind going too far too quickly. It would be too much to accuse the Agency of increasing the amount of taxes that *ought* to be paid, for example by changing laws. Such a statement risks moving us directly into the political sphere,[3] and the level of taxation in society is not a task for the Agency. It is there for all citizens, not only those who sympathize with the idea of increased governmental services and thus an increased tax burden. It seems like a backlash from the days when the Agency's emphasis was not on the right tax, but on collecting as much as possible. Successful work at the Agency in the 1980s–90s seemed to take place under the slogan 'the more tax collected, the merrier'. In those days there were even competitions between Agency offices, and the auditor who found most errors was a hero (Stridh and Wittberg 2015: 34). One auditor, Magnus, once reduced taxes by 200 million krona for a taxpayer, a result that dented his performance for the rest of the year. His nickname was 'Minus-Magnus' from then on (ibid.).

A literal reading of *more* tax risks banter; but I read this message as being that the Agency aims to increase tax compliance by following existing laws and underlining the inherent reciprocity in society. There are thus several issues at stake provoked by its aim to focus on strengthening reciprocity.

First, the belief that all other taxpayers pay more would not only increase total tax revenue but also make me as an individual taxpayer compare my increased contribution with others' perceived—increased—payments. There is a need to believe that others are treated the same way as I am. This does not necessarily mean that all taxpayers pay the same amount or percentage in tax. Countries have different tax systems for personal income: no tax, flat tax, regressive or progressive marginal taxes. Citizen's tax contributions might thus vary substantially; the issue for a tax collector is to make sure that equality applies in taxpayer treatment. A revenue collector should collect taxes according to democratically decided laws, rules and regulations.

The implication of equality is that the right tax for an individual is not necessarily more tax. There is thus a potential tension in Agency strategies between achieving the correct taxation for an individual and the aim on a societal level to, if not to close, then at least diminish the tax gap. If we are to believe the tax gap, these numbers indicate that the national tax take ought to be more than what is collected today (cf. Björklund Larsen 2017). There is a recognized lack of revenue; the issue is where and from whom to take it. The right tax must mean more tax on a societal level but not necessarily more tax for the individual. *More* means looking into forces that have impact on tax compliance.

Second, if others pay more—or less—the perception of payment is also directed towards on what and whom the increased governmental revenue expenditures will be spent. What treatment and provisions are other taxpayers given and what is their use of welfare (that we all pay into)? We have recognized a taxpayer's tit-for-tat relation to the state. The issue is *others'* tit-for-tat relation with the state vis-à-vis my own.

Third, the argument is that if a taxpayer expects to get *more* than s/he has provided, s/he is more prone to pay taxes. The *more* gets us quickly into the political sphere, as one can ask how much more in taxes we would like to pay and what other governmental services we would like to receive. Instead of concentrating on a reciprocal equilibrium, we get into a spiral of wanting more if we perceive we are paying more (cf. Hadenius 1985).

Therefore, to get something for tax money paid is something the Agency explicitly recognizes as important. In the large citizen survey from 2012, the question was posed for the first time about citizens' views on how tax revenues are used. The background for the question was that the Agency reasoned it was important for citizens to perceive that they get something for their contribution to tax payments, such perceptions being important in the long run (Skatteverket 2012: 24). Reciprocity was defined here in the sense of getting something for money paid in taxes and the impact of a direct reciprocal relation was compared with earning money *svart*; the Agency's argument was that there are certain public services that are only available if one is working within the formal, taxable economy, for example legal institutions such as courts and bailiffs but also in the case of formal bank loans and mortgages where a background check of yearly income is required. If a substantial amount of money is earned in the black economy, there is not much to show as income when dealing with the state's and society's formal institutions.

In this survey, citizens responded to the statement that 'tax revenue is well spent' thus: 37 per cent of respondents were neutral about the question, 8 per cent had no view, and the remaining respondents were dispersed equally between being positive and negative about the statement. The Agency's reflection on the result is somewhat ambiguous: it argued that such views could be both a healthy sign of citizens' engagement with how public institutions function and develop, but also a warning sign of discontentment with welfare spending (Skatteverket 2012: 27).

While these are examples of the explicit reciprocal relations with tax payments; there are also implicit ones. If less tax is paid there is less room for collective welfare services (Skatteverket 2012: 23). Indeed, 90 per cent of public income derives from taxation, so any decrease in tax revenue will diminish welfare services substantially.

In addition to the above explicit and implicit reciprocal relations perceived to exist between the taxpayers and the state, the Agency emphasizes a moral stance. Its current motto, prominently displayed on its website, reads *Vår vision är ett samhälle där alla vill göra rätt för sig* (Our vision is a society where everybody wants to pay one's dues and provide their fair share). This is a somewhat intriguing message as it emphasizes that the Agency is more than a mere collector of taxes but is a governing institution with a moral message for the members of state, the citizens.[4] Collecting the 'right tax' by making everybody paying their dues and providing a fair share is a strategy deemed to build legitimacy. The right tax is neither a specific number nor a maximizing amount, but ensures that each pays what s/he ought to. This is the equal treatment of citizens and legal entities. I have discussed this motto elsewhere in terms of the fairness that mirrors values in Swedish society (Björklund Larsen 2017), but elaborating further on this motto broadens our understanding of what is at stake.

A person who makes sure to always *göra rätt för sig* (pay one's dues) is also a trustworthy one. This person makes sure to provide and do what is expected, and will act according to norms and regulations in a given society. You can rely on work that is carried out by such a person as being solid and reliable; no corners will be cut. This person follows rules and regulations, not forgetting norms.

To contribute a 'fair share' can be seen as relational to all other members of society. It does not necessarily mean that everybody pays the same amount but that taxation practices are perceived as equitable and efficient among Swedes. Living, working and paying among the highest taxes in the world while also respecting the Agency that collects a large share of income is a considerable feat on the part of the Agency. And it is not only high taxes; taxes on income has high marginal rates. Personal income tax by international comparison is very high (cf. KPMG 2015) and constructed as marginal tax (with an increased percentage level on the last krona earned). High-income earners thus have higher tax rates than the average Swede, which means that the former pay considerably more for each 100 krona earned than do low-income earners (see also Chap. 4). Contributing a fair share has very different economic implications for Swedish taxpayers.

Finally, to *göra rätt för sig* also means to make sure that one is quits, at least at some point in time. Checking out from a hotel, paying for a restaurant meal, summing up several goods and services received are ways to *göra rätt för sig.*

The Agency thus balances its view of taxpayers as caring for society; implicit in the Agency's strategies is the message that taxpayers also ought to care for their own standing and be quits. Is there a tension here?

In the following we will scrutinize the *Limningers* and depict how they see their relationship to the state through their tax avoidance. If you recognize that an economy is based on reciprocity, you will never be quits; you will continue to be entangled (Thomas 1991). We will see here how recognizing reciprocity as one of the forces in the economy helps us to understand why *Limningers* sometimes avoid paying due taxes.

Getting Value for 'Tax' Money

Monika and I are having a coffee at a somewhat bland coffee shop on Limninge's main shopping street. We are seated in a pastel coloured yet nondescript room—striped wallpaper, laminate tables, Vienna-inspired chairs. Monika is a very quick-talking woman who is retraining to be an assistant nurse. It is a great job, she says, being with elderly people who are mostly so grateful and nice. In her previous job, she, together with her husband and a cousin, had continued the family business which she had helped out with since she was a child. As a teenager, I remember her with awe in this role from when I went shopping with my mother. She looked and acted so responsibly whereas I just stood beside my mother, seemingly useless. Monika and her kin had carried on the business until a few years ago, when they had been forced to close. It had been very hard work and long hours, and their business had become unprofitable owing to increasing imports and illicit competition (their competitors had used foreign workers remunerated *svart*). Changing career was the best thing she had done, she said.

Monika relates a lot to other Swedes and their respective situation in terms of why they buy *svart*. 'I can understand if you are very poor and try to cheat to get something extra. But not if you earn 25–30, even 40,000 a month. I don't think that you need to cheat then. That's petty.' She lifts her gaze to include all members of society, and adds:

> As an assistant nurse you are really badly paid and there is so much nagging and carping that Sweden does not have any money. A lot of people talk like that. Then you read in the newspaper the next day that the prime minister got a rise of 5000 more a month. I really think that it is too much of a difference. I can never imagine that they are worth that type of increase. That's what makes people so mad when they pay so much in taxes. (Björklund Larsen 2010: 191)

Monika is irritated about the income differences in society, but especially that what she pays in taxes contributes to economic inequality. She adds:

> I doubt there is anyone who questions that we should pay tax for good healthcare; you want to have good schools and dental care and that should be provided for. But it is all the other public expenditures [that people question]. If I knew that all my money went to something worthwhile, there is no limit to how much I would be willing to pay [in taxes]—if my taxes did not provide for strange things.

Monika is adamant that she should get value for taxes paid if she complies and they should not be spent on large salary increases for politicians. She was not alone in her views.

Anders runs his own plumbing business. It is a one-man shop located in a small industrial enclave of *Limninge*. He cares a lot about his business. Outside the entrance there are plants and inside it is clean and orderly. He has built up his firm by hard work and long hours. He asked me at least twenty questions up-front on my reasons for meeting him, who financed the project and so on. *Svart arbete* is illegal, so he is careful what he says. His business could be at risk, even if only talking about the small, yet illegal transactions 'that everybody else is doing'; the transactions for 'snuff money' as he calls them. I could feel his lingering question in the background: 'Imagine if the Agency chooses to make an example out of me.' Yet Anders decided to trust me, and gave me a good insight into his views on work and the environment in which he operates his one-man business.

We sit in his kitchenette, where he offers coffee and freshly baked pastries. Anders reasons along the same lines as Monika about the dishonest spending of tax revenue:

> It is enormous amounts [that are wasted. If I take] 1000 here or there, it is really nothing. If you see how these devils, these old men grab, those who should be role models, with their bloody travels. Look at the EU politicians, they trick here and there in order to get additional money when they travel, and in the end they travel the cheapest way anyway. In practice, you should be able to travel three times for the amount they get net [for each journey].

Although Anders fumes when he speaks about the frivolous expenditure of politicians, there are limits to what he can justify when earning *svart* money. He recalls the payment he received for a job done at some refurbished pizzerias. In his view it is not the money itself that makes it *svart* or not, but the amount and the context, which he illustrates by how it is carried around. A wallet belongs to an individual and there is not a lot of space in it. A briefcase, on the other hand, points to a more public environment. The briefcase can contain much more than the wallet and is usually carried around in professional settings. Larger amounts from informal transactions turn the operation into a business, a main activity that provides a livelihood. Anders did not say if the work he did for the pizzerias was with or without an invoice; just that he was paid in cash. Working too much *svart* professionally is not acceptable to him. As Anders explains, then you have to have a *svart låda*, literally a black box, somewhere in the firm. A black box makes for a separate economy, where informal incomes and informal expenses are kept. In these instances, there can be talk of an informal economy within a firm, which is separate from the public book-keeping and audits (Björklund Larsen 2010, 2013). Although he received snuff money, a large box was something Anders did not seem to want. But he knew very well how such a set-up would work.

Anders's latter explanations underscore the importance of taking a holistic view when we try to understand non-compliance. It is important to recall that reciprocal explanations are part of a larger reasoning. Although reciprocity can be borne in mind in one's understanding of how tax money is spent, there is also a simultaneous limit on how much can be justified in withholding tax that ought to be paid.

UNFAIRLY TREATED BY SOCIETY

This is obviously a personal stance: there are those who see avoiding taxes as a chance to get even. Surrounded by old fruit trees in full bloom, Larry and I balance on the old chairs in the lovely garden cafe of Högström's; it is difficult to find equilibrium on the uneven cobblestoned surface through which grass is fighting its way. It is early summer, a sunny day and a type of postcard setting for the nostalgic. What we are talking about is not very picturesque. Larry, who is employed with the coastguard, has many opinions on *svart arbete*:

> In certain cases I think [*svart arbete*] can be a sort of revenge ... against the government. One can see that there is cheating at higher levels, everywhere

from politicians at state level who take time off, you know within this system of parental leave and work amongst political party administrators. [Amounts of] money one can never imagine [are wasted]. So why shouldn't I do this if someone else can? I think these considerations stand for a large part [of why people buy *svart*].

Larry's previously relaxed and jovial tone disappears and he becomes rather agitated when in one go he justifies his purchasing and working *svart* as an opposition to the doings of the state.

Then it is the revenge bit, which is not anybody else's concern. This money, which comes straight in, well it feels a bit more fun for me to do something enjoyable with it. That [type of] money paid for my vacation for many years.

Niklas, a teacher, elaborates on why he thinks people cheat with taxes:

I just feel that ... no, I really thought about this with myself as a starting-point, I put myself into a hypothetical situation. I feel that if society had put me in the trash bin, they would not have helped me, and then I would feel that, what the hell, I don't care about it. I would act out of control, buying or working *svart* or whatever. That barrier is not important then. Because you do not feel any type of solidarity. I think it is like that. But, of course, where we draw the line differs amongst people.

Niklas is very careful not to buy *svart* himself; he does not like it. A person who is working *svart* puts her/himself in an insecure situation (not covered by laws, social security, etc.), he says, and this is not something he wants to contribute to.

When Johan tells me his story, he seems to be a prime example of Niklas's reasoning. Johan does not feel he has support from society at large and is deeply suspicious, vis-à-vis both authorities and society. He feels abandoned and betrayed. When I meet him, he is trying, unsuccessfully, to make a living as a tradesman. It is not a job he likes, but at the very least he says he can decide his own path. He has tried a lot of different jobs, among them a professional bass player in a rock band:

From the very start when we played, you know you are brought up with Olof Palme [former prime minister] constantly in the background. And somewhere, I had this guilty conscience about these *svart a* gigs. Maybe not so much, there were other things I had a worse conscience about. But it diminished over time, as there was no other way of getting gigs. They [the club owners] explained that there was just no alternative or they had to take another group. If they had paid social contributions, etc., there would only be a 50-note [kronas] left and you don't want that. Or you have to raise [the entrance] fees and that becomes impossible. But I've also had quite a few gigs *vitt* for that matter.

[My views] have changed over time, you get older and more interested in how society is run, and I voted a few times and thought a lot. Many things feel very strange and this [working and purchasing *svart*] has been a way of taking my distributive responsibility. I have large debts since my business was taken away from me. We were in the hands of an auditor and I did not get one *öre*. It was my big defeat then. I had tried to save the firm and somehow got the blame. It is not something I care about now; it doesn't bother me at all. The police couldn't do anything even if I called and nagged. So I trust my distributive ability a lot, a lot more than I trust Göran Persson's.

Johan embodies the welfare responsibility of the state in the then incumbent Prime Minister, Göran Persson. Johan feels betrayed, not only by the state but also by society at large. The state could not help him when he lost his firm and, when this is taken together with other defeats such as his fight for custody of his son, he feels alienated. This alienation is perceived in the Maussian sense of giving to society and not getting anything back (Graeber 2001: 162). Johan tells me that he has taken time out from society. He does not read the news or listen to the radio. Both the state and society owe him a debt, which is balanced back in his favour by his working and dealing *svart*. With this action he is able to justify that anything he earns is his and his alone.

BALANCING A FAIR DEAL WITH THE STATE

Although most *Limningers* support the idea of the Swedish welfare state and thus of paying taxes, there was always one way or another in which cheating could be justified in terms of a relationship to the state: a little less in taxes paid, inadequate welfare services or benefits, or the unwise usage and distribution of taxes paid. The *Limningers* quoted here might sound disappointed and disillusioned with the state of affairs. We should keep in mind that this is but one aspect of the justifications—although an important one.

Purchasing *svart arbete* as a way of dealing with the state hints at an ambiguity that concerns an individual discord between performing exchanges for private use and simultaneously acknowledging the (often perceived as negative) implications for society at large. Justifying these purchases thus involves negotiation between abiding by laws and regulations as a responsible citizen, and sometimes cheating with taxes—a balancing act. This balancing concerns taking back in order to settle what are considered to be outstanding debts. Keeping this balance is what makes purchases of *svart arbete* licit in the view of the *Limningers*. Yet justification in relation to the state takes place on a sliding scale.

At the one end of the scale, there is ample justification for a little bit of tax cheating in relation to the state. It is minding that my tax paid on a small salary goes towards politicians' large increases to already generous salaries or to their frivolous spending on, for example, expensive airfares. The tax money is thus not only badly spent; but it also goes towards making life easier for politicians through their private consumption. In a broader perspective, tax money is seen to finance a society which is unfairly constructed. Here we do not deal with immediate consumption and salary raises, but the tax money sustains a society where citizens are not treated in the same way as those in power. An ordinary citizen such as Larry, with some income here and there on the side, can compensate and, in his view, make his life somewhat better. Such money has paid for numerous vacations and made for a little golden edge to the otherwise ordinary life that a regular salary allows for. Then we have those who feel so badly treated by society at large that they want to log out—such as Johan. A regular job with tax payments and social benefits has never been had, and any attempts to create such a life have failed miserably. Johan feels justified in questioning why on earth he should contribute to a society that fails him—again and again.

In Johan's view, it is not only the state that fails; it is society at large that is not treating its members equally. In Chap. 4 we will come back to how a balance can be struck between other members of society; other taxpayers and their reluctance or willingness to comply with the taxes due.

The Agency advocates for a Swedish society where everybody should do their fair share: citizens contribute by paying taxes due; a tax collector makes fair and reasonable decisions when performing its fiscal duties; and institutions of the state spend the tax collected in an equitable way. Yet these Swedes that *gör rätt för sig* have given their view of society in terms of economic dealings with the state. They pay their dues and feel they provide their fair share, although they have explicitly withheld tax money in various ways.

Their relationship is pronounced as reciprocal. And this is where I would like Marcel Mauss to reenter the scene. From the gift giving between people creating reciprocal relations focusing on a specific gift, we can borrow from Mauss again, looking into a society as a 'system of total prestations'. It is a collective type of contract with fuzzier legal and economic concepts (Mauss 2016: 112). Taxes—'gifts'—circulate in this society with the certainty that what is given to the state guarantees a reciprocal action. The crucial distinction here is the time lapse between what is given and what is eventually received. A gift within a 'system of total prestations' cannot be immediately reciprocated, nor be postponed indefinitely. So it is with taxes paid.

Conclusion

To regard taxation in a modern democracy such as Sweden from a relational point of view casts a more nuanced light on the propensity to cheat with taxes. Life is not so simple that our motives for purchasing *svart* are purely economic or continue the way in which 'we have always exchanged'. Explanations are neither just poor excuses nor whitewashes; instead they illustrate how people can justify equalizing/balancing perceived outstanding obligations. This perceived expectation, I have argued, provides an excuse to balance the reciprocal relation. It is not a constant feeling, but emerges now and then as a justifying component. As such, it is a subjective valuation nourished by news, rumour, tales and habits.

With their justifications of informal purchases, many *Limningers* claimed there was an outstanding debt on the part of the state. It is perceived that the state owes them something, and as in their opinion the state is unable to pay this debt back, they take charge themselves and buy work informally. As such, 'buying *svart*' is an expression of an unequal reciprocal relationship with the state and its members. There are few who would like to buy everything *svart*; only the occasional transaction is acceptable as an attempt to even out an outstanding debt, to somewhat balance a reciprocal credit in their favour. This insight also underscores the need for taking a holistic view on citizens' tax compliance.

We have also seen a revenue-collecting bureaucracy that expresses views on a society peopled by citizens who wish to contribute their fair share and on the other hand citizens who balance their exchanges by tax cheating, in order to equalize their standing with the state. It is a game of perceptions, and the big challenge for the Swedish state is to maintain the perceived balance; that taxpayers get something for what they have given to the state.

In this chapter I have argued that a resident who lives, works and pays taxes in a state can to a certain extent define her/his bond with this state as reciprocal. Taking up Kerstin Jacobsson's cue that reciprocal exchanges provide the normative foundation on which the welfare state is based (Jacobsson 2006: 20) means that they give (pay taxes) in order to receive (welfare). It is a relationship defined by what the state compensates me and my kin with in relation to our contributions. Taxation is thus, as Mauss suggested, an example of a system of total prestation.

NOTES

1. Historic examples show that early on the state argued that revenues from tolls and other taxation on trading was to provide protection for merchants (cf. Hart 2005: 169). In sixteenth-century Sweden market trading was for a while just allowed in townships that were granted rights and these were only given if the burghers were seen to have fulfilled their duties towards the city they lived in (Staf 1935: 235).
2. *Det skall vara lätt att göra rätt och svärt att göra fel.* Note the difference between *göra rätt,* to do something correctly or to do something right thing, and *göra rätt för sig* which means to pay one's dues.
3. More tax paid means less (net) income to spend according to an individual's own wishes and needs, yet it could also imply better and more services.
4. Compare this message with the mottos of other Nordic tax authorities. The Norwegian *Skattetetaten* has adopted the motto 'to secure the welfare state's funding' and the Danish *SKAT* takes a slightly more moral stance, stating that taxes 'secure just and efficient financing of our future public sector'. If the mottos are mirrors of legitimate taxation values in society, they also cast light on 'what goes' in respective society.

LITERATURE

Aidt, Toke S. 2003. Economic Analysis of Corruption: A Survey. *The Economic Journal* 113 (491): F632–F652. http://onlinelibrary.wiley.com/doi/10.1046/j.0013-0133.2003.00171.x/full

Allingham, Michael G., and Agnar Sandmo. 1972. Income Tax Evasion: A Theoretical Analysis. *Journal of Public Economics* 1: 323–338. http://scholar.google.se/scholar?hl=sv&q=sandmo%2C+agnar&btnG=#0

Björklund Larsen, Lotta. 2010. *Illegal Yet Licit: Justifying Informal Purchases of Work in Contemporary Sweden.* ACTA UNIVE. Stockholm: Stockholm Studies in Social Anthropology N.S. 2. http://su.diva-portal.org/smash/record. jsf?pid=diva2:287414

———. 2013. Buy or Barter? Illegal Yet Licit Purchases of Work in Contemporary Sweden. *Focaal. Journal of Global and Historical Anthropology* 66: 75–87. http://www.ingentaconnect.com/content/berghahn/focaal/2013/00002013/00000066/art00008

———. 2017. *Shaping Taxpayers. Values in Action at the Swedish Tax Agency.* Oxford: Berghahn Books.

Borg, Per. 2008. Historiska Perspektiv På Skatte-Politikens Framtida Förutsättningar. *Underlag till Globaliseringsrådets Skattegrupp.* Underlag till Globaliseringsrådets Skattegrupp. Stockholm. http://scholar.google.se/schol ar?hl=sv&q=Historiska+perspektiv+på+skattepolitikens+framtida+förutsättnin gar&btnG=#0

Cowell, Frank. 1990. *Cheating the Government: The Economics of Evasion.* Cambridge, MA: MIT Press.

Daunton, Martin. 2001. *Trusting Leviathan: The Politics of Taxation in Britain, 1799–1914.* Cambridge: Cambridge University Press. https://www.google. com/books?hl=sv&lr=&id=DL2JYbnGkqQC&oi=fnd&pg=PR7&dq=daunton, +martin&ots=lag8igNyzC&sig=1chhD1NwLLsOT7cmwZYlJysv-1o

Drewry, Gavin. 2005. Citizens as Customers–Charters and the Contractualisation of Quality in Public Services. *Public Management Review* 7 (3): 321–340. https://www.public-admin.co.uk/brochures/cutomers_charters_paper.pdf

Ekman, Gösta. 2003a. Självdeklarationen 100 År. In *Deklarationen 100 år och andra tillbakablickar,* 7–20. Solna: Skatteverket.

———. 2003b. Några drag i den svenska skatteförvaltningens utveckling. In *Deklarationen 100 år och andra tillbakablickar,* 71–82. Solna: Skatteverket.

Ekonomistyrningsverket. 2012. Medborgares syn på myndigheter. *YouGov.* Stockholm: YouGov. http://www.esv.se/PageFiles/10647/medborgares-syn-pa-myndigheter.pdf

Engelbrecht, Sandra, and Sören Holmberg. 2012. *Svenskars bedömning av offent-liga myndigheters verksamhet* (Report 10). Göteborg: SOM institutet.

Falkinger, Josef. 1995. Tax Evasion, Consumption of Public Goods, and Fairness. *Journal of Economic Psychology* 16 (1): 63–72.

Folger, Robert G. 1986. Rethinking Equity Theory. In *Justice in Social Relations. Critical Issues in Social Justice,* ed. Hans Werner Bierhoff, Ronald L. Cohen, and Jerald Greenberg, 145–162. Springer US. http://link.springer.com/chapter/10.1007/978-1-4684-5059-0_8

Gouldner, Alvin W. 1960. The Norm of Reciprocity: A Preliminary Statement. *American Sociological Review* 25: 161–178. http://www.jstor.org/stable/2092623

Graeber, David. 2001. *Toward an Anthropological Theory of Value: The False Coin of Our Own Dreams.* New York: Palgrave Macmillan.

Guano, Emanuela. 2010. Taxpayers, Thieves, and the State: Fiscal Citizenship in Contemporary Italy. *Ethnos: Journal of Anthropology* 75 (4): 471–495.

Hadenius, Axel. 1985. Citizens Strike a Balance: Discontent with Taxes, Content with Spending. *Journal of Public Policy* 5 (3): 349–363. http://journals.cambridge.org/abstract_S0143814X00003159

Hart, Keith. 2005. "Money: one anthropologist's view." In James G. Carrier A Handbook of Economic Anthropology. Cheltenham, Edward Elgar.

Jacobsson, Kerstin. 2006. Durkheims Moralsociologi Och Välfärdsstaten. http://www.score.su.se/polopoly_fs/1.26584.1320939799!/20063.pdf

Johansson, Ove. 2003. Från undersåte till kund. In *Deklarationen 100 år och andra tillbakablickar*, 111–118. Solna: Skatteverket.

Kornhauser, Marjorie E. 2007. Tax Morale Approach to Compliance: Recommendations for the IRS, A. *Florida Tax Review* 8 (6): 599–634. http://heinonlinebackup.com/hol-cgi-bin/get_pdf.cgi?handle=hein.journals/ftaxr8&section=27

KPMG. 2015. 2015 Global Tax Rate Survey. https://assets.kpmg.com/content/dam/kpmg/pdf/2015/11/global-tax-rate-survey-2015-v2-web.pdf

Lepore, Jill. 2012. Tax Time. Why We Pay. *The New Yorker.* November 26, 2012. http://www.newyorker.com/magazine/2012/11/26/tax-time

Löwnertz, Susanne. 1983. De svenska skatternas historia: [En Artikelserie Av Susanne Löwnertz Tidigare Publicerad I RSV Info Åren 1982–83]. *Utbildning & Information.* Stockholm: Riksskatteverket (RSV).

———. 2003. Skattereformer För 100 År Sedan. In *Deklarationen 100 år och andra tillbakablickar*, 59–70. Solna: Skatteverket.

Magnus, Olaus. 1976 [1555]. *Historia Om de Nordiska Folken 1–4.* Hedemora: Gidlunds Förlag.

Malmer, Håkan. 2003. Granskningen av inkomstdeklarationer under 100 år. In *Deklarationen 100 år och andra tillbakablickar*, 21–58. Solna: Skatteverket.

Mauss, Marcel. 2016. *The Gift: Expanded Edition/Marcel Mauss; Selected, Annotated and Translated by Jane I. Guyer.* Chicago: Hau Books.

Narotzky, Susana, and Paz Moreno. 2002. Reciprocity's Dark Side: Negative Reciprocity, Morality and Social Reproduction. *Anthropological Theory* 2 (3): 281–305.

Odén, Birgitta. 1967. Naturaskatter och finanspolitik – ett finansiellt dilemma. *Scandia: Tidskrift för historisk forskning.* http://cts.lub.lu.se/ojs/index.php/scandia/article/view/779

Pardo, Italo. 1996. *Managing Existence in Naples: Morality, Action, and Structure.* Cambridge: Cambridge University Press.

Schumpeter, Joseph A. 1954. The Crisis of the Tax State. *International Economic Papers* 4: 5–38.

———. 2010. *Bemötande och förtroende.* Solna: Skatteverket.

———. 2012. *Medborgarnas synpunkter på skattesystemet, skattefusket och Skatteverkets kontroll. 1.* Solna: Skatteverket.

———. 2013. *The Swedish Tax Agency's Strategic Direction.* Solna: Skatteverket.

———. 2014. *Verksamhetsplan för Skatteverket.* Solna: Skatteverket.

Skatteverket. 2005. *Right From The Start.* Solna: Skatteverket.

Staf, Nils. 1935. *Marknad och möten.* Doktorsavhandling, Uppsala universitet.

Stridh, Anders, and Lennart Wittberg. 2015. *Från Fruktad Skattefogde till Omtyckt Servicemyndighet.* Solna: Skatteverket.

Svallfors, Stefan. 1996. *Välfärdsstatens moraliska ekonomi.* Umeå: Boréa.

Thärnström, Björn. 2003. Broschyren dags att deklarera under 30 År. In *Deklarationen 100 är och andra tillbakablickar,* 119–128. Solna: Skatteverket.

Thomas, Nicholas. 1991. *Entangled Objects: Exchange, Material Culture, and Colonialism in the Pacific.* Cambridge, MA: Harvard University Press. https://www.google.com/books?hl=sv&lr=&id=_HUfaBYEAOMC&oi=fnd&pg=PR11&dq=thomas+1991+anthropology+gift&ots=nlcSkmgqAc&sig=GhXODYgXbxlAr8dzAeb0l1mMw3E

CHAPTER 3

Taxpayer to Taxpayer Relation

Abstract To exchange and thus to create reciprocal relations is a human propensity and even a necessity for human solidarity. To exchange is an important aspect of what produces and maintains social relationships, and as such is one of the cornerstones in the making of society. But when Sweden has a law that says that all exchanges having value, regardless of how they are compensated, ought to be subject to tax assessment it becomes tricky. Do Swedes not exchange in private at all? Or are they all cheating when it comes to taxes? The Agency aims to increase compliance by stating that everybody should provide their fair share; then reciprocity, as a result of economic exchanges between citizens without involving the state, becomes problematic.

Keywords Barter • Private–public division • Informalization • Share economy • Copy-cat reciprocity • Legitimate taxation

To exchange and thus to create reciprocal relations is a human propensity and, as Mary Douglas emphasizes in the Foreword to *The Gift*, is a necessity for human solidarity (Mauss 2002 [1990]: xiii). To exchange is an important aspect of what produces and maintains social relationships, and as such is one of the cornerstones in the making of society (Davis 1992). But when Sweden has a law that says that all exchanges having value, regardless of how they are compensated, ought to be subject to tax

© The Author(s) 2018   75
L. Björklund Larsen, *A Fair Share of Tax*,
https://doi.org/10.1007/978-3-319-69772-7_3

assessment it becomes tricky. Do Swedes not exchange in private at all? Or are they all cheating when it comes to taxes?

These taxpayer to taxpayer relations are the subject of this chapter. We will continue to untangle the contemporary motto that steers the Agency's strategies in order to explore the insights it has about informal exchanges, for example those between taxpayers, where the state and its public institutions do not take part. When a risk analysis assessment project performed at the Agency showed that reality differed from previous messages reported about Swedish tax compliance, the resulting report was not disclosed (Björklund Larsen 2017). Its strategies were at risk. As one manager at the Agency commented on a presentation of the report: 'We have a problem when we say that most taxpayers provide their fair share when in reality they do not.'

As we will see, there are a number of intriguing implications in this very moral message coming from a 'mere' government bureaucracy, albeit an important cornerstone for the Swedish welfare state. That the Agency publishes such a motto means that it takes a position not only as a governmental bureaucracy, but also as a societal actor that engages in citizens' interrelations in order to achieve tax compliance. It has to do so given the tax law that governs personal income, but also because it recognizes that people who trust each other pay more willingly into a common treasury.

I find it important to make a distinction between society and state here. Simply put, a society is a group of people involved in social interaction (Latour 1984). These people can share the same geographical or social territory and adhere to similar cultural values. Societies are characterized by numerous relationships between individuals; a given society may be described by the specific arrangements of such relationships. A state on the other hand is peopled by subjects who live under a specific system of government. Such subjects are ruled by specific political institutions. People more or less voluntarily belong to societies (in the plural). Often society *is* the state, for example Swedish society, but societies are also clubs and other organizational structures of people who share the same interests, beliefs or values. People are usually subjects of one state, sometimes depending on laws and regulations governing citizenship, but often feeling adherence to many societies.

We will see how reciprocity as a result of economic exchanges between citizens becomes problematic for the Agency. In its aim to increase compliance by stating that everybody should provide their fair share, it is in *its* relation to the taxpayers; it is fulfilling its fiscal aim. Taking reciprocity between people seriously is a different matter. When people exchange without taking the state into consideration, do such exchanges become tax avoidance strategies if interpreting the law to the letter—which, as we will see, the Agency does if provoked.

Yet Swedes do exchange—a lot. This chapter is thus about the everyday exchanges between people; about the reciprocity invoked in exchanges that if the law is read to the letter ought to be subject to tax. We will see how people find the rigid interpretation of the law incredulous, and how the different relations they invoke make for justified engagement in *svart arbete*. As Ruben, who works in the judiciary, says: 'You know, I do not identify with the state. But I would not cheat on Svensson living next door, would I? But somehow he belongs to the state as well.'

THE AGENCY'S VIEW

People who perceive that their compatriots contribute pay taxes more willingly themselves. This insight is recognized and discussed across a wide range of disciplines. For example, economic psychologists have explored various components of equity theory and run experiments on the fair distribution of resources between taxpayers (cf. Folger 1986); economists delve into tax compliance as a gamble that is independent of loyalty, but instead is based on the willingness to pay that depends on risk taking (Cowell 1990; Falkinger 1995: 42); and legal scholars study the distribution of fairness in terms of the interpretation of laws (Gribnau 2015; Westerman 2014). Citizens assess their payments of taxes and fees not only in relation to what they as individuals receive from the state (as we saw in Chap. 2), but they also compare their contribution with their perceptions of what their fellow citizens pay—how they identify themselves as members of that group (cf. Taylor 2002).

The impact of this research is made visible in the Agency's motto,[1] prominently placed on its website and pointed out in its strategies and communication with Swedish society: 'Our vision is a society where everybody wants to do one's fair share.' We drilled down into this message in Chap. 2, to see that for the Agency Swedish society is synonymous with the state. Regardless of what a citizen thinks about taxes, what legal entity s/he occupies and what knowledge s/he holds, the Agency's message is that all individuals pay in order to contribute to the state. Or at least ought to pay; and this is what the Agency strives for—it is a vision after all.

The Agency's book *Right from the Start* (Skatteverket 2005) elaborates on this vision. The book had several aims: to provide input for internal discussions; to relate research and knowledge about the tax gap; to propose strategies to diminish the gap. It related contemporary research and knowledge about tax compliance, mainly from research into psychology and criminology.

According to the book, the Agency would increasingly focus not on the evaders, but on those who complied. The Agency identified research on what makes people follow rules and regulations—not only in tax research, but over a broader spectrum of how norms and behaviour are shaped. The book decisively took a step away from explaining tax compliance from a purely economic standpoint, stating that '[r]esearch clearly shows that financial incentive, as well as the risk of detection and punishment, is less important than the influence of norms and moral values' (Skatteverket 2005: 6), adding that there was 'nothing to indicate that the tax burden has any influence on the degree or extent of tax evasion' (ibid.: 7). It is the level of acceptance among taxpayers that matters. The Agency therefore saw one of the more important tasks of a tax administration to be influencing such norms (ibid.: 127). Instead of controlling and auditing *after* tax returns had been handed in and taxes paid, the Agency increasingly aimed to became proactive and to find measures that would make taxation more relevant 'right from the start'.

Reciprocity was one of the strongest norms identified in this work. The definition proposed was 'that people "repay" a certain kind of behaviour' (Skatteverket 2005: 6) and that '[a]n individual will choose to cooperate and to contribute to the common good if others are doing the same' (ibid.). But as we know by now, tax compliance is not only based on doing what others do; there is also the element of conditional cooperation. This means that attention is paid to the notion that 'the extent to which others also contribute triggers more or less cooperation and systematically influences the willingness to contribute' (Frey and Torgler 2007: 137). The Agency regards such norms developed through evolution and are both socially learnt and biologically inherited (Skatteverket 2005: 6), adding that it is not only taxation that is concerned with such norms.

Based on the belief that reciprocity can be seen as part of the history of mankind, it was important for the Agency not to be seen as an imposer of rigid control, detection and punishment if people were found to be avoiding taxation. The idea was to encourage compliance and thereby also create good role models. People comply because they regard the rules to be just and they try to follow them, not because they are afraid of being punished. *Try* is key here, as the Agency recognizes that tax laws, and its interpretations of those laws, are not always easy to apply in practice (Stridh and Wittberg 2015). Every taxpayer should to the largest extent be given help in order to comply. The result would be that they would trust that all other taxpayers were complying to the same extent. The Agency's compliance work was centred on collecting 'the right tax' from each taxpayer.

Simultaneously with the compilation of *Right from the Start*, a large analysis project on black work, *svart arbete*, took place at the Agency. According to the project leader, they were 'trying to do the puzzle' about *svart arbete* (cf. Björklund Larsen 2010: 10). Among many other findings, an estimate of 13 per cent of the workforce had participated in work that had been settled informally. This included 'reciprocal' services, which are those exchanged without monetary compensation. The estimates were based on an interview survey with people who said that they had performed work *svart*; two-thirds came from work performed for households and one-third was income from work done for other companies—informally. The Agency recognized the difficulty of pinning down such jobs with current review methods, and also stated that there was very little overlap with income found in audit controls (Skatteverket 2006: 61).[2] There was no exact definition of 'reciprocal services' given in the above estimate, but it clearly included barter (ibid.: 57).

Insights from these projects governed strategies for the next decade—on the one hand ensuring that all citizens were providing their fair share and fulfilling their obligations as taxpayers but on the other hand acknowledging insights from the project on *svart arbete* where proposals were made to simplify the tax system. The system was argued to be complicated, outdated and not in accordance with the general opinion of citizens (Skatteverket 2007).

This was in the mid 2000's and the strategy of creating role models, and thereby compliance, has been downplayed during the last years as the emphasis has increasingly been on making audit controls more visible. It is thought that audits should be more integrated into work with other system measures and communication strategies (Stridh and Wittberg 2015). There are taxpayers who do not comply, and when the Agency shows that they will be found and made to pay, societal tax compliance will *ceteris paribus* increase. Audit controls have historically been very expensive and cumbersome to carry out, but digitalization efforts at the Agency (as everywhere else in society) make them increasingly simple, at least on a screening level, as diverse digital methods such as scorecards and data-mining are applied to taxpayer information and annual returns. It is important to emphasize here that the Agency does not sample risky taxpayers based on defined categories such as gender, age, education or place of birth, but on combinations of what is said to be risky behaviour.[3] Looking for non-compliant taxpayers, the Agency is not interested in people's attributes but in their practices.

This way of looking at risky behaviour directs our scrutiny towards how exchanges are made—and especially on the relations that such exchanges are said to create.

Although the Agency recognized that creating and maintaining reciprocal relations between people plays a role in tax compliance, exchanges that are seen to create reciprocity are not something they pursue in practice. The values of barter ought to be assessed for tax, but the Agency recognizes the futility in pursuing such behaviour (Skatteverket 2006). As one manager at the Agency said: 'It is not the type of exchange we are interested in pursuing.'

Recall the law—all exchanges that have value, regardless of how they are remunerated, ought to be subject to tax assessment. Although hardly anyone declares the mundane exchanges that have value in their yearly tax return form, a former expert at the Agency wanted to test the rules.[4] His account underscores the fact that the Agency has to be strict when challenged and that the letter of the law must be observed.

The expert, let us call him Sven, declared an extra income of 250 krona on top of his income as an Agency employee in the obligatory annual income tax return. This was the estimated value of a dinner that his daughter had given him in return for babysitting his grandchild one evening when his daughter went to the cinema. He was subsequently taxed on this amount, a result he appealed against stating two objections. First was that the social relationship between the exchangers was very close; he received compensation from his daughter. In addition, the sum received was less than 1000 krona, an amount that was less than the lower limit of what needed to be declared at the time. This appeal was turned down on both counts in a three-page letter. The argument was twofold. First, the sum received could not be regarded as any other type of taxable income and was instead added to his professional salary (however, no social contributions needed to be paid as the amount was less than 1000 krona). Second, the fact that the relationship between the exchangers was between child and parent did not change the decision.

Obviously there are millions of exchanges like this taking place daily, and the majority of people do not pay the slightest attention to the fact that they ought to be subject to tax. These everyday exchanges where people help each other are a general, common, human fact, and such bartering creates, maintains and strengthens relations—including among Swedes.

The pertinent question for the Agency, and for tax compliance, is where you draw the line between taxable and non-taxable. How does a service become explicit tax cheating in the eyes of the Agency? Is it the extent of organization? The amount exchanged? The relationship between exchangers? Or when the relationship is assessed—before or after the exchange has taken place? Exchanges create relations, so it follows that these aspects are vital in order to understand issues that impact tax compliance.

Imagine a bloke next door who bikes a lot. He is also good at maintaining bikes; he takes care of his own, as well as his parents' and siblings' bikes. He knows the art of fixing flat tyres; he oils bikes to prevent squeaks, shrieks, and squeals; he wraps the handlebars; puts the chain back in place; changes worn brake pads—you name it. He does this for his family, friends, friends of friends, perhaps the entire neighbourhood. Perhaps you can knock on his door and ask him to do it, or it might be common knowledge that on Sunday afternoons as well as on Tuesday evenings he is usually there to help you out?

So when he has fixed a flat tyre, how do you compensate him? The bike fixer has clearly helped you with a service. Does he do this for nothing? Do you hand him a few 100 krona notes (the amount depending on how much time he took)?

These are tricky questions for the Agency, and it knows about these unclear borderline issues—especially when the work is performed in private. What is taxable, they ask rhetorically (Skatteverket 2008: 62). A child who helps out at home and gets compensation? Or a teenager who cuts the lawn—does it matter if this is done at home or at a neighbour's house? What about the plumber who helps his neighbour, an auditor, to paint his house and in return gets help with an application for a building permit? Or if the same plumber fixes the auditor's leaking pipe in return for help with his book-keeping (ibid.)?

The Agency thus clearly understands the challenge of drawing the line between taxable and non-taxable issues, bringing out age, relationship, type of work and professionalism in the exchanges performed—not to mention the type of compensation. The Agency is seldom very explicit about such a border, a fact that probably increases its legitimacy (Björklund Larsen 2017: 154).

Yet it reflects the Agency's knowledge about the types of exchanges most Swedes engage in. Most of the *Limningers* seem to know that exchanges with value ought to be subject to tax. Yet in some instances it is seen to be acceptable to avoid reporting such exchanges. In what follows, we will examine such instances and how people justify them. In all cases, reciprocity is invoked as justification.

BARTER

To facilitate and economize when exchanging things and services with each other, *Limningers*, and probably most other Swedes, barter.

Barter is a direct exchange of services or commodities without using a medium of exchange such as money, yet it involves an element of calculation. It has often been depicted as old-fashioned and primitive, a less sophisticated form of payment than cash. However, research into contemporary exchanges has brought the concept back into the limelight. It shows that bartering is done for a variety of reasons. People in general barter when they prefer not to use money (Humphrey and Hugh-Jones 1992), or to evade taxes and fees in general (Hart 2001). Citizens in the Soviet Union performed *blat* as a way of getting around the red tape (Ledeneva 1998); while *popolino* in a working-class section of Naples barter in order to avoid contact with the authorities (Pardo 1996). Barter can be organized with intermediate payments such as local currencies like Ithaca HOURS (Maurer 2005) and Local Exchange and Trading Systems (LETS) (Williams 2012) not to mention the exponentially growing sharing economy, where at least some of the exchanges taking place can be said to be barter (Schor 2016). Barters have often been depicted as non-reciprocal (Sahlins 1972) and performed on the same moral level as theft (Gregory 1994), involving minimal trust between exchangers with little impact on social relations (Zelizer 2005). Yet barter usually occurs between people who already know each other, among family and friends, neighbours, colleagues, professional networks, or are made to feel they do so, facilitated by ratings in the digital sharing economy.

So people opt to barter and help each other for manifold reasons. It can be a habit, a way of being friendly, to build and maintain relations both political and ideological; but also because it is cheaper than buying (the calculation element being more pronounced). The exchangers already have a certain amount of trust as they help each other; barter is a practice that can take place outside the formal market and the auspices of the state. Money is therefore not needed as remuneration; a service is performed in exchange and the substantial amount of tax due can be avoided. In the Swedish context, it becomes *svart arbete*—one of those widespread practices that challenge laws, rules and norms. Acknowledged as wrong, it is in many instances acceptable. These exchanges highlight the inadequacies of the formal economy, which are pragmatically resolved by the actors who are subject to it (Björklund Larsen 2013a).

In order to understand bartering the entire value system in which the barter takes place has to be appraised (Humphrey and Hugh-Jones 1992: 15). An important attribute of the Swedish institution of barter is that taxation makes the exchange of services much, much more expensive. Barter is a means of economizing.

Björn, a trucker, exemplifies the impact of the difference between the costs for formal and informal work in a straightforward way:

> I think you should have it one to one. With what you earn for an hour of work, you should be able to pay someone else to do things you do not have time to do. But it is not like that today. You earn 100 krona and what's left is 50. With that you have to pay 200 for someone to come and do something for an hour. That's not fun. If you were to pay him formally, you would have to pay yet another 100. It does not feel OK.

Settling a deal by bartering can of course be more complicated than paying cash, as the worth of service and/or product has to be estimated by other means than in an equivalent monetary comparison. The objects exchanged are often different, and it seems of no great concern if one of the providers gets a bit 'more' than the other. The difference is that the calculation relates to what the services would have cost on the official market with invoices, taxes and fees included. A painter can exchange work (for private use) with an electrician. Even if time spent is not equal, both can be content with the outcome of the deal, as having to buy the services would have cost three to four times what their respective work effort was worth net. For those with skills to offer, bartering is much more economical than purchase.

Talking about barter in terms of closer relations lets Swedes justify those purchases that they know ought to be subject to tax. Barter is clearly made more licit than buying a service *svart*, regardless of whether the reason for the purchase is pure survival, not having enough money or attempting to get a service performed as cheaply as possible. There are also those who have no knowledge to offer as a barter, thus making cash payment the only alternative (usually higher educated people without practical skills). However, such a justification is trickier, since if money alone is used for compensation, a quite clear division between the licit and the illicit exchange is drawn. In the following we will see diverse examples of Limningers who justify their *svart* purchases by talking about them as barter. Closeness of relations, the extent of organization, scope of exchange and value calculated make exchanges more or less licit, but even when the deals are settled with money ideas of barter can be invoked (cf. Björklund Larsen 2013a).

Taxpayer Views on Barter

Discussing the proximity of relations and if 'helping out' ought to be subject for tax assessment, Pelle, an engineer, tells me about his uncle who gathered close family and other relatives during a weekend for a 'painting party' at his newly built house. Pelle asks rhetorically: 'Should that be seen as illegal? There are probably a few who would insist that it is *svart arbete*. I would never agree with that.' All the relatives helped to paint, and when it was finished they were invited to a good meal. In this case Pelle's uncle used family relations to get work done while simultaneously saving money. The outcome was probably that social relations in the family were strengthened while a fun event was created from tedious painting. One could see this as pure bartering—they got a meal after all—but more explicitly it is an expression of maintaining closer relationships. In this family we help each other and we have fun together; too bad if such services are also worth some money and could thus be seen as taxable.

A monetarily settled service makes for increasingly illicit types of *svart arbete*. Sometimes even those can be considered licit, which I shall return to later. Pelle voices what many said when he distinguishes between *svart arbete* and bartering services. He says: 'If a friend of mine is excellent at doing one thing and I, on the other hand, at doing something else, we exchange time with each other. For example, I am good at tiling and he helps me nail. That's definitely not *svart arbete*, whereas it is when you exchange your working time for money.'

Knowing the relation to the provider of the work is vital if it is to be seen as taxable or not. The Limningers almost spoke in chorus. 'If we are friends or family, then it is definitely not *svart*,' says Carl Johan. Hasse: 'It should not be taxed if it's mates doing the work. If I fix his garden and he my car. Which really [according to the law] is *svart*.' Janne points out that these are things that keep people together; not everything that he needs should be bought on the market. Most *Limningers* recognized the inherent problem of drawing the line between what is a help between friends, family and people in general, and what on the other hand can be considered *svart*.

Jenny, a hospital cleaner, muses on the border: 'There is a fine line between *svart arbete* and bartering services for something in return. Which I really think is a good idea. You know, if I am good at something and you at something else, can't we barter services? And not an *öre* is exchanged.' She gets really excited at the thought, but also raises a warning: 'You cannot do this as you like, not for big amounts of money. The value cannot be too high.' What becomes with this reasoning, is that helping each other becomes almost a bad thing, at least in relation to the state.

BUSINESS AND PRIVATE LIFE

Self-employed people know that they ought to draw a distinct line between business and private costs; in reality it can be quite difficult but may also provide manifold instances of getting things cheaper—much cheaper. This means that certain transactions are made more reciprocal than they really are. 'There is no one who only barters, it would be criminal then,' says Sten, who runs a small furniture store. 'It is done in small proportions, bartering products with each other. For example, there is this shoe merchant I know; I get a pair of shoes from him and he gets a chair in return.'

Sten points to this relationship in bartering with his fellow shopkeepers. He needs a pair of shoes. The value of these is (mentally) jotted down by his acquaintance who sells shoes. At a later date, he finds a chair to his liking, the price of which Sten in his turn notes somewhere. If the values of shoes and chair are fairly equivalent the deal is closed, even if the relationship with the counterpart is not (cf. Graeber 2001: 220). Any outstanding debt that has not been settled for some time they resolve with a more practical cash payment. An exchange that is beneficial for both thus maintains acquaintances and friendships, but is still concealed from the rest of society.

Tomas lives outside Limninge in a refurbished summer home with a neat, tidy garden. In one corner of the garden is an outdoor wooden spa tub, in another a pretty shed for garden tools. How this shed was built is an illustrative example of how one can barter through one's professional network. Tomas is a self-employed craftsman who works at many building and construction sites. He meets many people, has an extensive network to draw on and sometimes uses his professional relations to acquire materials for private use. When we talk about his involvement in *svart arbete*, he hesitates a bit and then says:

> There is a shed up there. Now I am being really honest, it hasn't cost me many krona. I have exchanged services for materials. I've been at one building enterprise here and another there. 'So I ask, there is a stack of bricks behind there, are you going to use them?' 'No, they are left over from the construction of those forty apartments.' 'It is just about what I need for the garden shed I am about to build. If I just charge half for that control report I did, can I take those bricks?' 'Yes, you just take them. They will be got rid of anyway.' There are those types of examples.

Tomas used his professional knowledge to acquire materials for private use, basically for nothing, through customer relations. Not only are the objects dissimilar, but he also barters a service for a commodity. The relation between Tomas and the site manager is based on professional dealings, yet it is probably strengthened by having made a smart deal with a reduced invoice exchanged for a stack of bricks. This hidden barter is concealed in order to avoid taxation. It is an unequal exchange converted into a strict monetary value, as those bricks have a different use-value for the construction company than they have for Tomas. For the construction company they imply a cost, as they have to be taken away as rubbish, whereas for Tomas those bricks have the same market value as if he had bought them from a store. In addition, he did not have to spend time going to a store, buying them and bringing them home.

That such situations occur is known by the Agency. In the risk assessment project performed by them, a similar result for small business entities was discussed, although here the issue was faulty cost deductions. The analysts probed into the question holistically: why do such costs occur; how common are they; how much do they amount to (as part of a tax gap measure)?[5] We saw Tomas barter products for reduced invoices in a transaction that was really a 'purchase' intended for private use but was mentally accounted for as part of his business activities. The barter was obviously cheaper, much cheaper (bought for non-taxed money without VAT), but it was also for many other reasons a good deal for both exchangers.

Exchanges that take place in private as opposed to on the public arena (when at least one of the parties is acting in the role of a business entity or in another formal role) are usually said to make for a different relationship. Yet when the Agency thinks about such cost deductions among professionals, they draw on results from audit controls that show these entanglements are more common than the Agency imagined in its strategies stating that most pay their fair share.

The analysts discussed this repeatedly. Lacke provided numerous examples. 'When the neighbour borrows a business-owned trailer, it becomes a type of societal grease. Taxwise it is usage of a business asset (and thus subject for tax assessment).' Susanna added: 'There are so many situations when people buy assets for the business, yet assets that are used to help the family or friends. Then we start going beyond family members.' Where is the line drawn between legal and illegal? When each purchase could be thought of as either business or as private, it can be tempting to justify them all as business-related costs.

An Example: Horse Trotting

One issue of concern at the Agency that was repeatedly discussed was horse management. It is expensive and there are large economic incentives to incorporate such a hobby into other business activities, which would allow expenses to be deducted. Historically, horses have been used for a number of tasks in Sweden but are contemporarily viewed as a hobby for the elite, thus being deemed exclusive.[6] From this point of view, owning horses sits badly with the idea of an equal Swedish society, yet not all 300,000 horses in Sweden are used for upper-class activities.

Greger, a factory worker, lives in a forested area in the south-east of Sweden where he has built a house next door to his grandparents' farm. He uses the attached stables to breed and train trotting horses, his big interest. There is nothing exclusive about Greger's homestead, yet he loves working with the horses, so his part-time factory employment is a way to survive. He has bred and trained at least ten horses, yet he cannot survive on what they bring in.

Greger barters—a lot—and not only in relation to his horse activities. In the trotting community, there is a lot of bartering going on, he says, as so many who are active there have very limited means. At home he exemplifies barter with the job he does with his excavator. He digs for his neighbour, but does not declare what he gets for it as an income. When I ask if it is money he gets, he replies: 'Sometimes. Most often he does something for me instead.' And he adds: 'It is not legal, you know.' So he barters, as do many other horse breeders, in order to be able to continue with his big hobby. Greger is yet another example of how people talk about exchanging services as barter; it is not always barter but it is talked about as such.

Back to the Agency and the risk assessment project. One issue that analysts thought would be subject to much cost deductions were the so-called hobby firms. To distinguish hobby activities from self-employment is a major concern of the Agency, which suspects that many citizens wish to register their hobby as a business activity,[7] in order to facilitate the deduction of costs. In the risk assessment project, many considerations were made to distinguish between activities that can be referred to as hobbies and those that are viewed as commerce or industrial activities. The reason for this is that many hobby activities are expensive; if you can make them look commercial they can be transformed into a loss-making activity and therefore deductible (Björklund Larsen 2015). This idea came to nought; the random audit control could not identify any hobby firms. They probably exist, but among the firms sampled for the audit they passed under the radar.

BUSINESS AND PRIVATE LIFE CONTINUED

For the self-employed it is in practice difficult to separate business and private transactions, and this is also recognized by the Agency. There are so many instances where these spheres overlap in everyday practices that exchanges made in private—supposedly increasing reciprocity—are accounted for as a business activity in the market sphere, thereby creating less reciprocity.

Larry, a coastguard who is very able with his hands, reflects on this. When he started out working, there was always someone among his colleagues who had to do some work on his house, and all of the colleagues helped out. 'There were electricians, painters, carpenters—the lot. And everyone knew that next year it was someone else's turn and a few weeks would be spent there. This just organized itself without anyone commanding.' In Larry's story, there is a nostalgic, old-time camaraderie— men who gather in the summer, laughing and cracking jokes while making a veranda, an extension to the summerhouse or installing a new kitchen.

Yet when a group of professionals refurbishes a house for a client such bartering is not possible among the workmen. It becomes *svart* work. Even if the intention is not to make it cheaper for the owner of the house—the client—this work is carried out by the workmen in their professional role. Such work is too organized and all transactions should be formal. There are various informal ways of exchanging work and things between the professionals that in the end have consequences on the tax system—usually the result being less tax collected. Monetary gains are not everything; a reason for not invoicing among the network of craftsmen can also be to avoid the extra administration it creates. It is boring and cumbersome, so it is easier to remember small favours and recompense them at some later stage.

The Agency says it understands the challenges in administrating VAT and invoices appropriately. As for cost deductions, there is always the challenge of determining if such costs have been used professionally or in private. This is meticulous, even nit-picky work and makes for the negotiation of many subjective evaluations. Instead of evaluating and arguing over such issues both internally and with the taxpayer in question, would it not be easier to apply a flat tax deduction, as most other countries do? The opportunity to invoke reciprocity in such cost deductions would be erased. The project manager, Lars, proposed that this issue should be looked into as part of the analysis work, to see if countries with flat tax deductions avoided the continuous evaluation problem that was encountered at small business audits.

It was of no use. A flat rate deduction would be much easier to explain and to administer, yet it was considered a non-question at the Agency. Gunnar, the manager at the analysis department explains why:

> It is not seen as fair. The Swedish basic taxation principle is 'after each one's ability'. Any legal proposals have always carried some sort of tax adjustment rules.[8] Many other countries have flat rate deductions; these are easier to control but more unfair, and our political climate does not allow for them. We have to tax according to accumulated profit. Imagine a restaurant in the countryside and compare it to one in the Stockholm centre. How would you apply a flat rate tax and make it fair? I have seen many attempts but it just doesn't work here.

INFORMALIZING THE FORMAL

Ruben talks about *svart arbete* as an ongoing process, interacting with the state's increasing involvement in its inhabitants' daily activities:

> The state, those in power, well, we have a larger control of citizens than we had fifty years ago. Way back then it was not that kind of [societal] construction. *Svart* did not exist. Now everything we do ought to be known. I think

it [*svart arbete*] by definition has increased, because there is more control today [and thus ways of measuring lost tax revenues]. But go back fifty or a hundred years and apply the same template as we have today. I do not think it has increased; we just did not think in those terms then.

And he continues with an example which is still in existence today, but only in sectors with unaccountable waste, such as restaurants and fresh food providers:

Well, hell, if you had a grocery in the 1950s, if you needed five kg of butter to bake on a Saturday you just took it home. Today, it ought to be taxed; otherwise it is wrong. It wasn't like that before. That's why it [*svart arbete*] has increased by definition.

Ruben reflects on how the state is seen as having more insight into households' economies, and at the same time more explicitly separates the private from the public. Larissa Adler Lomnitz (1988) aptly described the interrelation between the formalization of systems and people's responses which take the form of increasingly informal activities. She argued that, with the growing bureaucratic formalization of exchanges in society, there will be a similar growth in informal mechanisms which might mirror the increase in Swedish *svart arbete*. Although strengthening the relations within such groups, these informal activities fracture society (ibid.: 53). In the Swedish context, we can see loose-knit networks of craftsmen, for example those that Larry, the coastguard, and Tomas, the craftsman, referred to. They help each other in reciprocal networks, omitting the state and also taxes, fees and so on.

Informal purchases of work can be a result of adaptations to laws and regulations which are perceived to be contradictory. With perceived increased incongruities in laws and regulations, the cheating can expand. Lars sees *svart arbete* as a result of this. He works within the construction sector and is (as seen earlier) positive with regard to the *svart* practices as a criticism of the state:

The [political] majority is incredible. I mean, the sector where I work is sensitive to political decisions. So now they are back, these ROT deductions.[9] For a period VAT was differentiated between materials and work. No fool would then buy materials, just a bloody lot of working hours. Then you had to fool around with that type of nonsense.

What Lars was referring to was the change of wording on invoices, minimizing the costs for materials and changing as much as possible to become work—which is then subsidized. The increasing formalization of society (Adler Lomnitz 1988), for example through the 'explosion of rules' (Ahrne and Brunsson 2004), was able to provide a background for how the possibilities for transacting *svart arbete* also increase. It does not erase *svart arbete*, just makes it look different.

Informal transactions of work flourish not only between people who are socially related or within interest-based groups. Instead they can almost become the norm, feasible between complete strangers. Swedes wanting to acquire a service *svart* rarely have a problem finding one. *Limningers* who want to buy services *svart* only need to ask cautiously, in ambiguous language: I don't need an invoice, but can I get a jolly good price or can you do it at the weekend?

Börje sums up what many seem to believe. People have always exchanged. It's a natural part of life:

> You fix this and I'll fix that. But I do not think that's working *svart*, although it is in the grey zone. If you are tough [on interpreting the law]. I think it's congenial with this market trade. Because that's what it is. It's exchanging all the time, either exchanging services or exchanging money; whether there are goods or services. They have always existed and will always exist. You can never do away with this legally.

FORMALIZING THE INFORMAL: SHARE ECONOMY

There are exceptions. Mona, a midwife, says that it does not feel as if we want to share and care like we used to. Society is harder, more inhuman, she says. People care less and less for other people, except for those at the very core and the immediate family. She is convinced that this climate of uncaring has a larger impact than we would like to admit. It creeps in, she says: in the beginning people might object, then you get accustomed and used to it, and thus accommodate this egoistic feeling.

If we buy into Mona's reasoning, it is valid to question if the centennial tax law as well as the rise of the sharing economy was a sign of the times; that it reflected a society where fewer and fewer people 'care' about each other. The law that was seen as successful at the time (cf. Lodin 2011) both politically and in its legal construction turned a blind eye to people's need for everyday exchanging. All of a sudden a lot of exchanges that previously had been barter became *svart arbete*. Barter rings were for a time seen as an alternative—with no money involved—but these were quelled when the Agency recognized in a writ that all exchanges taking place within a barter ring or any other type of organized exchanges ought to be subject to taxation (Skatteverket 2009b; cf. Björklund Larsen 2013a).

Organized bartering has existed for a long time, with Ithaca HOURS (Maurer 2005) and LETS (Williams 2012) being just two examples. What can be considered barter has recently expanded into the flourishing arena of exchanges in the so-called sharing economy.

This proliferation has been greatly helped by society's increased digitization and the abundance of web- and app-based applications. Sharing economy practices have increased for a number of reasons: it is practical to share, as you do not have to own or maintain things; it is more economical for the same reason; it is sustainable as not so many things have to be produced and can be used more widely; and it can solve allocation problems, such as getting a ride in sparsely populated neighbourhoods (Alexius et al. 2017). Not all of the so-called sharing economy practices can be defined as creating reciprocal relations: Airbnb and Uber might disguise themselves in 'sharing terms', but their endeavours are driven by plain commercial interests. Theirs are just two of many instances in the sharing economy where corporations take on the role of a broker: Airbnb and Uber are intermediaries providing digital platforms where a person in need can find (underused) services and things offered by other private persons.

From these various examples—yes, most exchanges can create some type of relation. At one end of the continuum of exchanges that create relations there is altruistic helping and sharing; at the other extreme there are pure market exchanges. When does an exchange become sharing instead of expecting something in return (Widlok 2013)? Thomas Widlok proposed that it is the motive to give that is lacking. The act of sharing is done for its own sake (ibid.: 16); it is a complex form of interactions that starts with a demand rather than an offering (ibid.: 22).

Regardless of intentions and reasons for sharing and bartering, the Agency has a definite stance on what is taxable or not (Skatteverket 2009b, 2016). Depending on the status of the provider of the service/thing—self-employed or private person—income from the sharing economy is taxable to the same extent as any other income, and the type of recompense does not matter (Skatteverket 2016: 17).

The inherent properties of *how* services are exchanged are one challenge for the Agency. Participation in the sharing economy increases tax errors (Skatteverket 2016: 4). It is both more difficult to declare income from 'sharing something' as the rules are complicated, and when income is difficult to account for there are obviously problems in controlling and auditing such activities. The Agency is cautious regarding the sharing economy. It does not advocate for changing legislation, but raises concerns about the erosion of traditional roles: customer–provider; investor–project owner; employer–employee; lender–borrower. Who reports what to the Agency is not as clear cut in the sharing economy. The implication is that the sharing economy challenges the Agency's strategy; that on the one hand it should be easy to report, and pay, the right tax, and on the other hand it should be difficult to err. The Agency does not have the right tools and administrative routines to handle the sharing economy. Tax matters here direct the limelight away from the law itself and onto the application and practice of the law at the Agency as regards these new exchange practices.

The problems with correct tax in the sharing economy that the Agency points to are not new. It is in the new forms of bartering; the explosive increase of such exchanges being helped by the new digital platforms.[10]

From an Agency perspective, it is when the calculative and organizational element in bartering kicks in that such exchanges become taxable. The Agency cannot overlook such exchanges any more in the way it could when they were less organized, scattered and performed through informal networks (yet not barter rings; see above). Such services are performed for a variety of reasons, yet their public organization makes all of them subject to tax. It is a fair nation we live in, is it not—where all are treated equitably?

The sharing economy illustrates that the way in which exchanges are performed between private persons will not necessarily make relations better. However, the feedback offered for a certain service makes *who* the provider is more explicit. The ratings demanded by participants that are so essential for digital platforms provide a constant negotiation of relations between exchangers. Someone with good ratings is a person you inherently trust and will use for a service. The proliferation of good exchanges makes for successful participation in the sharing economy.

Yet shared things can also be socially attractive as they sustain social cohesion in neighbourhoods. We share with and thereby care for our community, while also brokering a good deal (Björklund Larsen 2013b).

CONCLUSION

Following Mary Douglas's initial concerns about human solidarity being created by exchanging, it is valid to ask whether such solidarity is possible in Sweden with the current tax law in place. If Börje is right about that people have always exchanged, to change people's behaviour is not that easy for the state, especially if they have to pay more dearly for it. But as we have seen, the Agency has actually succeeded in implementing a simplified tax system while also concealing issues that are difficult to legitimize. Most importantly they aim to treat people equitably. This increases reciprocity.

Like most other people in the world Swedes continuously exchange. Yet direct exchanges between people keep the state outside the deal. Such exchanges are justifiable among the *Limningers* as long as they are not too organized or happen too often, do not have too much value, are not performed by professionals in their working time or by a complete stranger. When *Limningers* talk about cash payments for informal purchases, it is the small and almost negligible amounts that are acceptable; aspects of unacceptability appear in the size of the deal, the type of recompense and the organizational form. The *Limningers* know about the law, but don't pay too much attention to it if certain conditions are in place. The acceptable purchase of *svart arbete* is private and hidden, but set against a public reference to what constitutes economic activities.

For example, bartering, in the sense of keeping money out of the deal, makes the direct exchanges more acceptable. Yet even if money is sometimes used, there are many ways to justify this, for example by invoking a closer relationship. Settling the exchange with money makes the links to market and state more pertinent, and the *svart* deal becomes more explicitly an act of cheating. Therefore, even cash-settled deals are often referred to as barters in order to create a reverse disentanglement, away from the formal market and closer to the realm of social exchange.

The Agency seems to go along with this—unless provoked, as it was with Sven's, the employee expert, test of limits before an exchange was recognized as taxable. What he tested was how close the relationship between exchangers can be and how small a value the exchange can amount to. In this case the Agency read the law to the letter, but it mostly let such exchanges pass. As seen above, it knows that there is a myriad of exchanges that ought to be subject to tax assessment according to a strict interpretation of the law. For various reasons these exchanges should not be subject to tax: they are not publicly spoken about, as it would be seen as an intrusion into people's everyday lives; these exchanges create and maintain reciprocal relations among citizens; and if assessed for tax they would threaten the Agency's legitimacy. I propose that the Agency actually increases its legitimacy by interpreting the law 'generously' and instead focusing on making sure that all taxpayers are treated equally and made to do what all others are doing. Tax compliance is then achieved as a copy-cat and equality reciprocal relation. This is also why horse management can be viewed somewhat suspiciously. It is deemed an activity for the privileged and thus sits badly with the idea of Swedish equality.

Notes

1. It is noteworthy that the Agency only collects taxes; it has nothing to do with their (re)distribution.
2. These estimates were obtained through extrapolation of interview survey methods, and I take that reciprocity here implies being paid in kind.
3. Presentation by Andreas Voxberg, Business Intelligence Expert at the Agency. 5.8.2016.
4. See also Björklund Larsen (2010: 141) for a comparative interpretation of this event.
5. What initially seemed like quite simple questions became quite encompassing when the analysts developed their thinking. Finally, they stated five questions:

   1. Are the regulations and the legal framework unclear? Here we can draw upon compliance work looking at the law itself and how the Agency has interpreted the law and developed it into regulations and information to be followed.
   2. Studying how common the obvious faulty deductions are is an attempt to quantify the existence of such faults among the Swedish population at large. These quantifications could for example become part of the tax gap calculations.
   3. The question of how other taxable entities are affected directs attention towards the legitimacy of the Agency. If taxpayers believe that other citizens pay their dues, they will continue to comply with what they owe.
   4. What are the consequences resulting from the rapid expansion of the self-employed? This question builds on the replies to the previous questions and thus prepares for the more encompassing and final question.
   5. How to identify the risks (to the Agency) from these deductions? (Björklund Larsen 2017: 81–82).

6. The Agency has devoted a lengthy, in-depth writ to the difference between a hobby and commercial activity (Skatteverket 2009a, Writ 131 342327-09/111).

7. The government has been encouraging entrepreneurship by facilitating the registration of small corporations or as self-employment. It is a very easy task to complete, but a follow-up is lacking. Such registrations have also been abused for various types of dubious economic activities.

8. In Swedish, *jämkningsregler.*

9. ROT (*reparationer, ombyggnad, tillbyggnad*—repairs, refurbishing, attachments) subsidies have been used now and then to boost the building industry, in times of a slack economy. These subsidies could be used for certain types of reconstruction work at private homes with tax deductions up to a given amount.

10. PricewaterhouseCoopers has estimated the value of the sharing economy globally at 123 billion krona; by 2025 the amount will be 2740 billion. Although these are guesstimates, most actors seem convinced that the sharing economy is here to stay and will take up an increasingly large proportion of services exchanged. The production industry will most probably be challenged by increased usage of existing products, but that discussion is for another forum.

LITERATURE

Adler Lomnitz, Larissa. 1988. Informal Exchange Networks in Formal Systems: A Theoretical Model. *American Anthropologist* 90 (1): 42–55.

Ahrne, Göran, and Niels Brunsson. 2004. Regelexplosionen. In *Regelexplosionen*, ed. Göran Ahrne and Nils Brunsson, 199–220. Stockholm: EFI, Stockholm School of Economics.

Alexius, Susanna, et al. 2017. Fler behöver bry sig om delningsekonomin! Accessed May 10, 2017. http://digitalutmaning.se/wp-content/uploads/2016/12/Ett-dokument-om-delningsekonomin-slutversion.pdf

Björklund Larsen, Lotta. 2010. *Illegal yet Licit: Justifying Informal Purchases of Work in Contemporary Sweden.* ACTA UNIVE. Stockholm: Stockholm Studies in Social Anthropology N.S. 2. http://su.diva-portal.org/smash/record.jsf?pid=diva2:287414

———. 2013a. Buy or Barter? Illegal yet Licit Purchases of Work in Contemporary Sweden. *Focaal Journal of Global and Historical Anthropology* 66: 75–87. http://www.ingentaconnect.com/content/berghahn/focaal/2013/00002013/00000066/art00008

———. 2013b. Moulding Knowledge into a Legal Complex: Para-Ethnography at the Swedish Tax Agency. *Journal of Business Anthropology* 2: 209–231. http://ej.lib.cbs.dk/index.php/jba/article/view/4159

———. 2015. 'Common Sense' at the Swedish Tax Agency. Transactional Boundaries Separating Taxable and Tax-Free Income. *Critical Perspectives on Accounting* 31: 75–89.

————. 2017. *Shaping Taxpayers. Values in Action at the Swedish Tax Agency.* Oxford: Berghahn Books.

Cowell, Frank. 1990. *Cheating the Government: The Economics of Evasion.* Cambridge, MA: MIT Press.

Davis, John. 1992. *Exchange.* Minneapolis: University of Minnesota Press.

Falkinger, Josef. 1995. Tax Evasion, Consumption of Public Goods, and Fairness. *Journal of Economic Psychology* 16 (1): 63–72.

Folger, Robert G. 1986. Rethinking Equity Theory. In *Justice in Social Relations. Critical Issues in Social Justice*, ed. Hans Werner Bierhoff, Ronald L. Cohen, and Jerald Greenberg, 145–162. Springer US. http://link.springer.com/chapter/10.1007/978-1-4684-5059-0_8

Frey, Bruno S., and Benno Torgler. 2007. Tax Morale and Conditional Cooperation. *Journal of Comparative Economics* 35: 136–159. http://www.sciencedirect.com/science/article/pii/S0147596706000849

Graeber, David. 2001. *Toward an Anthropological Theory of Value: The False Coin of Our Own Dreams.* New York: Palgrave Macmillan.

Gregory, C.A. 1994. Exchange and Reciprocity. *Companion Encyclopaedia of Anthropology*: 911–939.

Gribnau, Hans. 2015. Taxation, Reciprocity and Communicative Regulation. *Tilburg Law Review* 20: 191–212. http://booksandjournals.brillonline.com/content/journals/10.1163/22112596-02002009

Hart, Keith. 2001. Informal Economy. In *International Encyclopaedia of Social and Behavioural Sciences*, 845–846. Oxford: Elsevier.

Humphrey, Caroline, and Stephen Hugh-Jones. 1992. Introduction: Barter, Exchange and Value. In *Barter, Exchange, and Value: An Anthropological Approach*, ed. C. Humphrey and S. Hugh-Jones, 1–20. Cambridge: Cambridge University Press.

Latour, Bruno. 2015. The Powers of Association. The Sociological Review 32 (1_suppl):264–280.

————. 2006. Purchasing and Performing Undeclared Work in Sweden. Part 1: Results from Various Studies. Solna: Skatteverket.

Ledeneva, A.V. 1998. *Russia's Economy of Favours: Blat, Networking, and Informal Exchange.* Cambridge University Press.

Lodin, Sven-Olof. 2011. *The Making of Tax Law: The Development of the Swedish Tax System.* Amsterdam: Iustus Förlag AB. http://www.ibfd.org/IBFD-Products/Making-Tax-Law-Development-Swedish-Tax-System

Maurer, Bill. 2005. *Mutual Life, Limited: Islamic Banking, Alternative Currencies, Lateral Reason.* Princeton, NJ: Princeton University Press.

Mauss, Marcel. 2002 [1990]. *The Gift.* London: Routledge.

Pardo, Italo. 1996. *Managing Existence in Naples: Morality, Action, and Structure.* Cambridge: Cambridge University Press.

Sahlins, Marshall D. 1972. *Stone Age Economics.* London: Routledge.

Schor, Juliet. 2016. Debating the Sharing Economy. *Journal of Self-Governance and Management Economics* 4 (3): 7–22. https://www.ceeol.com/content-files/document-431329.pdf

Skatteverket. 2005. *Right from the Start.* Solna: Skatteverket.

———. 2007. *Svartköp och svartjobb i Sverige. Del 2: Möjliga åtgärder mot svartarbete och bidragsfusk.* Solna: Skatteverket.

———. 2008. *Mätning av skatteverkets effekter på dess omgivning.* Solna: Skatteverket.

———. 2009a. Hästverksamhet – gränsdragningen mellan hobby- och närings-verksamhet. Writ 131 342327-09/111. Solna: Skatteverket.

———. 2009b. Beskattning av medlem i bytesring. Writ 131 319224-09/111. Solna: Skatteverket.

———. 2016. *Delningsekonomi. kartläggning och analys av delningsekonomins påverkan på skattesystemet* (Rapport 131 129 651-16/113).

Stridh, Anders, and Lennart Wittberg. 2015. *Från Fruktad Skattefogde till Omtyckt Servicemyndighet.* Solna: Skatteverket.

Taylor, Natalie. 2002. Understanding Tax Payer Attitudes through Understanding Taxpayer Identities. In *Taxing Democracy: Understanding Tax Avoidance and Evasion,* ed. Valerie A. Braithwaite, 71–92. Aldershot: Ashgate Publishing, Ltd.

Westerman, Pauline. 2014. Reciprocity: A Fragile Equilibrium. *Netherlands Journal of Legal Philosophy* 2 (43): 172–184.

Widlok, Thomas. 2013. Allowing Others to Take What Is Valued. *HAU: Journal of Ethnographic Theory* 3 (2): 11–31.

Williams, Colin C. 2012. The New Barter Economy: An Appraisal of Local Exchange and Trading Systems (LETS). *Journal of Public Policy* 16 (1): 85–101.

Zelizer, Viviana. 2005. *The Purchase of Intimacy.* Princeton, NJ: Princeton University Press.

CHAPTER 4

Tensions between Paying and Receiving

Abstract If reciprocity defines the relation between exchangers in society, its quality is also decided by how much has been given and received. Getting too much demeans the recipient in relation to the provider if the recipient is unable to give/pay back; it creates a feeling of inferiority. Conversely, the one who provides more than others can pride her/himself as being *magister*. In a fair and equal society, the other side of feeling *magister* provides the possibility of evening out perceived injustices. The 'Pillars of Society' and the 'Balance Artists' believe in the welfare state, and each provide their version of a fair share. It is a perception game in terms of paying/avoiding/evading taxation that is addressed as contributive and distributive balancing acts.

Keywords Being magister • Marginal taxation • *Fair share* reciprocity • Pillars of society • Balance artists • Contributive and distributive balancing

BEING *MAGISTER*

If reciprocity defines the relationship between exchangers in society, its quality is also decided by how much has been given and received. Getting too much demeans the recipient in relation to the provider if the recipient is unable to give/pay back; it creates a feeling of inferiority and the one

© The Author(s) 2018   99
L. Björklund Larsen, *A Fair Share of Tax*,
https://doi.org/10.1007/978-3-319-69772-7_4

obtaining too much has the least status (Mauss 2002 [1990]: 48). Previous chapters have hinted at such tensions.

Conversely, the one who provides more than others can view her/himself with pride. S/he is a *magister*, a person with authority whom others look up to (Mauss 2002 [1990]: 95). Having paid the most gives one the upper hand in relation to the other person. The gift has implications when a citizen articulates a reciprocal relation with the state if s/he perceives that s/he has given more than s/he has received. How does the feeling of being *magister* work out in a society where ideas about equality are said to be profound?

This chapter raises the other side of feeling *magister*—that it also provides the possibility of evening out perceived injustices. Instead of feeling superior for having paid more in tax in relation to other citizens, the perception of having paid too much makes for ample justification for avoiding taxes in other ways. The inherent challenge in reciprocal relations is here clearly pronounced. If we get the same we should also give the same; if others pay the same they should also get the same. You can even out perceived imbalances, but if you do not pay although you ought to and take although you ought not to, this is below the acceptable level of behaviour.

In this chapter you will get to know the Pillars of Society and the Balance Artists, those who believe in the welfare state and in various fashions provide their fair share, but also have strategies to make sure that it is fair. When they have paid too much, they find ways to even out the perceived status of being *magister*; when others have not paid enough, this provides the same basis for reasoning. You will also become acquainted with those who have checked out of society; who do not want to either to give to or take from society.

This perception game in terms of paying/avoiding/evading taxation will be addressed as contributive and distributive balancing acts. The emphasis will be on the *Limningers* and their reasoning about balancing. There are certainly differing opinions at the Agency about why citizens avoid taxes. Although it is recognized that both environment and context have a large impact on behaviour (e.g. tax avoidance), the Agency has no intention of judging citizens' motives or morals (Skatteverket 2015) Wisely, they state that they have no idea why people make errors; the only thing they can do is to diminish the possibility of erring as much as possible.

Progressive Marginal Tax

Among the *Limningers*, one of the most common explanations for the existence of *svart arbete* is the Swedish tax rate, which is perceived as very high by international standards. The *Limningers* have diverse opinions on the reasons for this, but they almost reached a consensus when talking about taxes. Hasse: 'I think you feel like that. With the world's highest taxes, if you get the chance, I think you will cheat, yes you will.'

Sweden is among the top contenders for the highest taxation in the world and has a system of marginal tax on personal income. Marginal tax rates are usually applied to income in countries with progressive taxation schemes, with incremental increases in income being taxed in progressively higher tax brackets. Applying progressive marginal tax rates means that high-income earners pay a larger percentage on the last krona earned than do people with a lower income.[1] Overall, it also means that the former pay a larger proportion of their total income in tax than those with less income. This is not taking any subsidies or tax deductions into account (see below for an example).

Compare this with a flat tax, or proportional tax, where all income is taxed at the same percentage, regardless of amount. An example is a sales tax, where all purchases are taxed at the same percentage.

Applying a higher marginal tax rate on high incomes is thus one way to redistribute income in society. There are different views about how progressive marginal tax rates impact the willingness to do extra work, acquire additional education or strive for increased income and career benefits. It is therefore in doubt if and how the progressive marginal tax rates have an impact on national fiscal income (e.g. Flood 2015). If the largest part of an increased salary rise goes to tax, the question is to what extent people will strive for better incomes and *ceteris paribus* pay more taxes (not as a percentage but as an overall contribution). Choosing the 'right' level between income distribution and net tax revenue seems to be an eternal question in the Swedish political debate on taxation.

The Nordic countries, together with Belgium, are usually considered as having the highest marginal tax rates, although Sweden has a particular history of a period with exorbitant marginal tax rates, this culminating in 1976. When Astrid Lindgren (author of the Pippi Longstocking books and many, many other children's stories) discovered that she paid 102 per cent in taxes, she wrote a satirical saga, *Pomperipossa i Monismanien*, published in one of Sweden's largest tabloids (Lindgren 1976).

In a clear allegory, the story is about the witch Pomperipossa who resides in a lovely country far, far away, where she writes children's books. She cares for all her compatriots, as well as for the politicians who have managed to create a society where everybody gets a fair share of the welfare cake. Pomperipossa is happy to participate in baking this cake, contributing more as she earns quite a lot more than the average resident. Yet one year she is told that she will pay 102 per cent in marginal tax. Although she is an author, she knows that so many per cent do not exist! In passing, Lindgren mentions that she can lower her taxes by buying a large house borrowing a lot of money (interest rates were at the time tax deductible and such purchases were used to lower taxes among higher income earners). This was a pinprick to Sweden's incumbent Minister of Finance, Gunnar Sträng, who had just purchased such a house and could therefore, despite being a high-income earner, lower his taxes. Sträng responded that Lindgren's contribution to the tax debate displayed 'a strong unsatisfactory knowledge' about the tax system, 'although we do not require Astrid Lindgren to have such knowledge'. Lindgren responded by giving an interview on the radio the following day, saying that she 'thought that Gunnar Sträng had understood the tax system. But if there is someone who cannot calculate, it is the National Tax Agency, *Riksskatteverket*; they have sent me the numbers. Sträng can tell stories, but he clearly cannot count. Perhaps we should change jobs, him and me?' The story of Pomperipossa and the discussion about taxes is said to be a contributing factor to the loss of power by the Social Democrats in the 1976 parliamentary elections—their first loss in forty years. Although Swedes are said to be compliant, there is a limit even for them.

It is a long time since these excessive marginal rates were in place, yet Sweden continues to have high marginal tax rates. Most people do not object to the idea, although there is a heated discussion about the percentages (Björklund Larsen 2017: 9). Income redistribution via progressive marginal taxes is hardly questioned publicly; it is not *comme il faut*. In private, however, there are many who express qualms about living with the high tax burden the Swedish variety of marginal taxation implies.

Looking at the other side of taxation—the provision of welfare benefits—the same questions can be asked. If individuals who receive means tested benefits see them decreased if more income is earned, what is their motive to earn more? This is sometimes described as an implicit marginal tax rate. It is not in doubt that these issues can create a disincentive for work or promotion and may result in a structural income inequality, as some economists argue—the question is to what extent.

These issues are not peculiar to Sweden, but are seemingly a common feeling throughout the world: that people feel they are paying more than they get for it (cf. Laurin 1986). The amount of tax on work as part of gross national product (GNP) has a high correlation with *svart arbete* (Skatteverket 2006a: 222). Viktoria, who runs her own business, says:

> Of course you connect the tax-rate level with *svart* money. That is, it is clear to a five-year-old, a teenager—in any case a young grown-up person—that there is some sort of balancing going on. That people and companies try to avoid the taxation rules [when taxes are so high].

Susanne, a public relations (PR) manager, says that she is convinced that we are taxed to pieces in Sweden. People are really fed up with paying taxes on everything, she says. That's why they buy *svart*. With the level of tax, there are some who express a feeling that anything which can be taxed will be:

> For goodness sake, you shouldn't pay taxes for something you have already paid for with taxed money. You can't pay taxes on taxes, it is stupid. That's how it is with the gas [for the car]. You pay VAT on it. That's tax on taxes. The [cost of] gas is only a third of what you pay. When you take things like this into consideration, I really think working *svart* is fine. We don't protest enough in Sweden. We just clench our fist in our pocket and go on.

Lars obviously does not have much regard for the current state of taxation policies in Sweden. Almost everyone I talked to referred to this one-sided preponderance. Their narratives make up a chorus of annoyed voices, not peculiar to Sweden although easy to voice here, in a nation that has among the world's highest taxes.

PILLARS OF SOCIETY

Despite these voices of non-compliance, most *Limningers* actually like and are proud of the welfare state they live in and contribute to. Hasse, a gardener, exemplifies this when he says that he and his wife must be considered model inhabitants, *samhällsbärare*, Pillars of Society. He pictures himself as a victim who carries the load of others, but somewhat unwillingly.

Notions of the Greek god Atlas being punished come to mind. The carrier of society does not, unlike Atlas, carry the weight of heaven and earth himself, but shares the burden with a few others who provide more welfare than they receive within society. Situationally the *samhällsbärare* can even bring to mind the task of Sisyphus, in the sense that he never seems to benefit from his input to the welfare state. He works and pays his taxes, is hardly ever sick and does not use many of the services provided by the welfare state. So Hasse is proud. He could probably count the sick days of his entire working life on his fingers, and thus infers that he is a net contributor to the welfare state. He works and pays taxes, in contrast to others whom he points out are net recipients, for example those who receive sickness benefits.

Samhällsbärarna (plural) is a category also used by the Agency for those who do not buy *svart* (Skatteverket 2006b: 33).[2] *Samhällsbärarna* are, in the Agency's depiction, paid less and are less educated than the average Swede; they are mostly women or people placed outside the formal labour market such as students and retired people. These people cannot afford to purchase services formally, but also have fewer needs as they do not own many things; their housing is mostly rental. They are considered very moral in their relation to the state—and as the Agency points out it is not problematic for them to be moral considering that they have fewer assets and thus less need to maintain them. *Samhällsbärarna* follow laws and regulations and have socialistic leanings. Needless to say, they are much in favour of the Swedish welfare state (Skatteverket 2006a: 174).

What is implicitly assumed to be *svart* in the Agency's statement above refers only to private purchases of services from professionals. A pillar supports something and the *samhällsbärare* in the Agency's depiction certainly embrace values that uphold the Swedish welfare state. Yet in terms of financial contributions to society—taxes—this group's support is more modest. The Agency's notion of *samhällsbärare* takes on the moralistic tone of strictly law-abiding citizens. This is different from Hasse, who thinks he is fulfilling his commitment to a good, but slightly unjust, society. Hasse is quite content with life, but he wishes there were more people like him. It is important for him to perceive himself as a net contributor. When he works *svart*—it is always small amounts and at a set price—he points out that he *helps* other people. While out working, there is often someone in the neighbourhood turning up to ask for help in his garden. It could be cutting down a tree, cutting a hedge or putting some paving stones in place. It takes a few hours, he says, but as he gets older he does such jobs less often. He regards his small involvement in *svart arbete* as compensation for his overall surplus contributions to society.

Bo can also be regarded as a *samhällsbärare*, although he differs from the Agency's definition in most aspects except in his moral stance. Bo is an information technology (IT) engineer and has the position of a director at one of the larger Swedish corporations. 'I definitely do not like *svartjobb*,' he says. 'I think you have to show solidarity with the state. I am definitely not a Social Democrat … I earn a lot of money and pay an awful lot in taxes, but I really feel it is my duty to do so.' To pay more than one receives in return has been described as an expression of a reciprocal regime of status (Ledeneva 1998: 150). Such a person is powerful and has an extensive network of connections. They can offer favours that are more or less impossible to reciprocate; thus is their position in society affirmed (ibid.: 153). He is *magister*: having paid the most gives him the upper hand in relation to others.

Bo is proud of providing more than he gets. He relaxes by working on his summerhouse; he built it more or less himself, he proudly explains. The issues he could not deal with—electricity, plumbing—he bought; with an invoice, it is underscored. He thought quite a bit about what an acceptable purchase of *svart arbete* could be, knowing what the law states. 'It has to be the occasional, unplanned recompense,' he says, adding:

> When you give something in return—not directly, mind you—for the unexpected help or from someone you are very close to. The intention is important and such transactions can never be organized. When a craftsman expects the work he does to be paid without an invoice, well then it is unacceptable; then the work becomes *svart*.

An emphasis on giving more to society than one takes from it is the fundamental trait of these *samhällsbärare*.

BALANCE ARTISTS

Unlike the Pillars of Society, the Balance Artist has a more nuanced reciprocal relationship with the state and society in which s/he lives (cf. Björklund Larsen 2011). S/he must perceive a balance between what s/he pays and what s/he gets back from the state, and this can be achieved in various ways.

The reasoning is that there is just too much given to the state. VAT on goods and services is too high, and too large a part of earned income is paid in tax; the state just takes too much of what is perceived as belonging to the private sphere. However, balancing can also work the opposite way, as we saw in Chap. 2. The state's priorities are wrong and the fiscal revenue is spent in an irresponsible way; on administrative expenses and in particular on the perception that public employees get too much—wages are too high, travel is too expensive, there are too many fringe benefits of a sort that the common employee does not enjoy in his working life.

Börje is a typical Balance Artist. He basically thinks that society is good, but when he encounters unfair treatment, he reacts to it (cf. Björklund Larsen 2013: 425). The needs of ordinary people are not understood by the state, or more specifically by the politicians and bureaucrats ruling the state from Stockholm. So Börje pays his tax through his usual employment as a logician at a major international IT company. In addition he works *svart*, telling me that 'he has hammered on quite a lot of houses'. For his services, he has received various materials. There has never been any money as recompense, he says, instead he has picked up some stuff here and there as compensation for helping to build garages and so on. There are so many friends, he says, a great network of acquaintances who know what he can do. And they always find something to offer in return for his services.

CONTRIBUTIVE AND DISTRIBUTIVE BALANCING

So how is it that some people, for example those who consider themselves to be Pillars of Society, believe in the state to such an extent that they are willing to provide more in taxes than they ever expect to get back? Why do we see 'the surrender of individual chances of survival or economic gain, for the sake of an advantage that accrues to all within a given collective, regardless of their own contribution' (de Swaan 1988: 25)? De Swaan argues that this is not a paradox, but should instead be viewed as a transitional movement. People have an expectation that most of those deemed members of the community will collaborate, and thus contribute. As this is a transitional state of affairs, it implies that they can abandon this effort when it suits them better—for example to buy *svart*. They are 'calculating entrepreneurs' in the welfare state (de Swaan 1988: 229)? Yes, they calculate, but not only for their own economic benefit. The *Limningers* mostly believe in and are proud of their welfare state; there are just certain individuals and specific governmental practices that promote the incorrect spending of tax revenue. A citizen can do little to correct such practices, so instead s/he can be said to vote informally with her/his wallet to fix such wrong-doings. This is elaborate thinking about the contribution and distribution of tax money, but the notion of 'calculating entrepreneurs' puts too much emphasis on market practices. Although there are elements of calculation in the *Limmingers*' reasoning, I suggest that 'balancing' is a more appropriate concept.

Balancing is a perceived notion of equalizing something which is tilting to one side or the other. Think of an old-fashioned market scale with too much weight in one of its bowls, or a see-saw with a larger child sitting firmly at ground level with the smaller child left hanging in the air. Balancing is used here to underscore a process of continuous giving and taking. You will never be quit (Thomas 1991).

Gauging a balance can be described as involving what is exchanged with what is received in return. If these seem equal, the exchange relation is balanced (Befu 1977: 269). This is what takes place within the reciprocal transaction, not through one specific trade but accumulated over time through manifold transactions. When you balance you keep an equilibrium over time; this does not have to be instantaneous, but when the chance arises you take it. As exchangers seldom value what they exchange in exactly the same way (cf. Slater 2002), including social issues can allow these exchanges to be perceived as a 'positive-sum game' (Befu 1977: 270). Perception is, of course, crucial here. What is of value for one person does not necessarily have the same value for someone else, as we have already seen in various ways.

It needs to be emphasized that the purchaser's strategy of maintaining a balance is not with the supplier. The acceptable purchase of *svart arbete* is voluntary in the sense of agreeing to the transaction with the provider, and the resulting reciprocity taken into account here lies in its relation with the state. It is an imaginary balance, obviously not possible to calculate in numbers but in terms of a discernment of evenness and thus of no less importance.

There are two sides to balancing and engaging; with Mauss, it could be said to consist of reasons for giving and taking. The giving side balances what are perceived as contributions. These are feelings such as I have paid too much money, devoted too much time or conferred too much knowledge already. In short, I have given too much. It also means that others have not done their share, for example by cheating with taxes (which I, of course, have already paid).

Larry effortlessly lists a few synonyms for *svart arbete*, which leads him on to reflect on the state:

> *Svart*, black, *utan kvitto*, without receipt, *vid sidan om*, on the side, or should some of the payment go to Stockholm? Well, I think I said this once. I have sent far too much money to Stockholm. It [talking like this with a customer] was like having a mutual enemy all of a sudden. It was so much easier then.

The justifications for evading taxes are thus manifold, and finding a common justification for why a transaction should be cheaper puts the exchangers in a good mood. Both transactors have done a good deal and saved money for something else, so the reciprocity created by the transaction makes them feel they have slightly balanced out the relationship to the state. It is about getting even—that others who have cheated and been smart are now on a more equal footing. The common enemy is those in power—located in Stockholm, the capital. It should be pointed out that the state is in some sense an imagined foe, as in reality most of the income taxes paid are for, and used by, the local municipality. Only higher incomes are subject to state taxes, whereas VAT and other non-income taxes are for redistribution by the state.

These practices are called *contributive balancing*. This is based on the reaction to a state that is seen as taking too high a portion of income, and takes place in opposition to the enforced collection of taxes. Viktoria, eloquent and very opinionated about taxes and their impact on society, says what most other people expressed in one way or another as she brings up the contrarian balancing—that what has been paid in taxes is unwisely spent, and intentional or not, public decision-makers do not measure up to the task of redistributing all this money. In this view, taxes paid should provide something in return:

> I think that people generally are very irritated that efficiency is so low in society, without being able to put it into words. We are constantly fed news by the media about politicians taking out increasingly higher wages, at the same time arguing for the general pay level to be kept at bay. They get apartments and golden handshakes. Morale diminishes, of course [she laughs], if

the role models do not practise as they preach. I do not have anything against paying taxes, but I get irritated over not getting more for them [the taxes].

Viktoria's reasoning supports the result of a study about the attitudes of Swedes to cheating with taxes. The majority, 65 per cent, justified their behaviour with the response 'because people in important positions break norms of society' (Skatteverket 2006b: 39). Thus, if powerful people seem to do wrong, then the ordinary citizen, *Svensson*, makes up for it when the opportunity arises. Purchasers of *svart arbete* do not want to pay their dues to the state, because others—who have more—do not, or because they take out more than they should. These are people who could be described as 'free riders' (Svallfors 1996: 36).

These feelings are reinforced from the opposite side, the 'taking side'; distributive balancing. Here, justification concerns others taking or getting too much—those not deemed deserving. Examples are politicians and bureaucrats who use money unwisely; badly, inefficiently, selectively—either for their own benefit or for a specific group of other people. Other illustrations could be citizens who make claims they are not entitled to in terms of subsidies, using social insurance unjustly or claiming unemployment benefits while working (often *svart*). The distributive balancing seldom originates from direct examples, but rather through rumours, the media and diverse interpretations of reports and evaluations.

There are thus different reciprocal relationships at play here. First of all, what taxes are spent on is seen as relevant. Swedish income tax starts at quite low income levels. Most people pay a high proportional rate, but if they are in need there are different subsidies in compensation. If these taxes are seen to be spent 'frivolously', such as high incomes and remuneration for government employees, the informants deem it immoral behaviour. Ordinary taxpayers have worked hard for their incomes and struggle on their own to make ends meet. Seeing taxes spent unwisely hurts. Monika, for example, illustrated her point with absurd incomes and rises for bureaucrats and officials in Chap. 2.

Viktoria sees it from the same point of view:

Well, actually, I imagine that people think the state is cheating them. I think the general perception is that the state cheats them for so and so many krona in taxes. So what do I get for the amount paid? Well, one part goes to all the politicians with their increasingly high wages, to those who are members of committees and boards and get compensated for a few hours of work. And then they get pensions in ten years for one year of work. It is such a tremendously big difference compared with a regular salaried employee. They are not that many, but this doesn't matter because they are the role models. It is a bit like cheating people for money, I think that people's morals ... well, many justify theirs, they don't cheat in return but they justify their *svart* payments and recompense. They think they earn it; they have paid so much but have not got the yield they deserve.

Anita has a similar opinion: —'As things are now, when you read about those high positioned civil servants and politicians who line their pockets in different ways, it gets more acceptable to do it. If they can take a share, why shouldn't I, an ordinary person?' While these practices among the supposed role models continue, *svart arbete* will continue to exist. Staffan reinforces this view:

It is not that strange that there is such an effect. That's how you reason when you see role models in society—politicians, high-positioned civil servants, corporate leaders—who take their share in an absurd way and even break laws and regulations. I am convinced that they have an effect on people in general. They think, if the role models can, so can I.[3]

Is there a difference between complaining about contributive versus distributive balancing in analytical terms? If there are perceptions of paying too much, there will also be expectations of getting as much back. On the other hand, getting very little from the state also means that the willingness to contribute is even less. It could be put as a question about the chicken and egg, but in terms of a reciprocal relation it is rather about how the Maori proverb was originally translated: 'Give as much as you take, all shall be very well' (Mauss 2002 [1990]: 91). Mauss pointed out in a footnote that the wording is rather 'as much as Maru gives, so much Maru takes and this is good, good' (ibid.: 189).

Larry further illuminates contributive versus distributive reciprocity. 'They cheat me everywhere, so I take a little bit in return. I minimise the damage. I would like to see those who decide, those in power.' He hesitates, and brings to mind a 'commercial' that was shown in cinemas at the time of the interviews. This film clip, paid for by the Agency, shows a decrepit neighbourhood with run-down high-rise buildings, giving an image of a poor ghetto where unemployed no-good youths are running around, mostly spending time having a go at what there is left to trash. Larry describes seeing this advertisement and reflects on it:

You know, when you go to the movies and see some commercial with the message that it is cool to pay taxes and then they push over some park bench. I can understand that, in the best of worlds, it would be perfect. But whom do Swedes cheat, then?

I ask if he is referring to the Agency's film clip, and he nods and continues:

I've been doing jobs for people who work at the Agency. 'Imagine if they knew about this', these people say and chuckle. So for a moment ... OK, who should be most ashamed in this instance? Maybe I, who have been so nasty as to ask? I don't know.

This 'informative' film clip was one of the strategies to increase tax compliance, and was a warning of what would happen if Swedes did not continue to contribute (compare with the earlier messages from the finance department in the 1950s as described in Chap. 1). Society will deteriorate into declining suburbs drained of regular citizens and Pillars of Society; it cannot continue to maintain a welfare state for those most in need. Redistribution will suffer, and images from poor areas of the Bronx or the riots in Paris's immigrant suburbs come to mind. These images threaten the idea of the Swedish well-kept, stable and safe People's Home, *folkhemmet*, a somewhat ethnocentric pride.

Larry's justifications highlight the tension between giving and taking. He does not contribute when earning money *svart* through the work he performs outside his ordinary employment; but neither do the purchasers. They ought to pay VAT as well as a higher price to Larry if the money he earns is to cover social fees and taxes. The purchasers avoid contributing, although they work collecting and organizing tax contributions. This again highlights the difference between private and public roles and the respective purchases one makes in each. If those working to collect citizens' contributions do not live according to the rules and laws, who does? When Larry meets the enforcers of the tax laws who wish to purchase *svart* for their private use, he cannot help wondering about the moral contradictions between acting in public and private roles.

Citizens assess the transfers not only in relation to the state, but also in relation to other residents—they compare their contribution with perceptions of what fellow citizens pay, and receive.

To analyse tax compliance, and cheating, as a reciprocal feeling focuses our attention on the relationship between exchangers, not only in a dyadic sense, but as part of the larger community to which they feel they belong. A citizen who lives, works and pays taxes can to a certain extent define her/his bond to the state in terms of reciprocity, of having certain expectations. It is a relationship defined by what the state compensates me and my family with in relation to our contributions, but also compared with what other members of the state, the other inhabitants, are perceived to contribute and receive respectively. With Swedes striving for equality, this also means that it is important for them to keep this relationship in balance, even if this results in the state's occasional deception. In some cases, it may even result in their seeing themselves as 'being in the black', as it were.

NOT PAYING FOR THOSE WHO DO NOT PAY

There are the 'double takers', sitting high upon the see-saw. Those who do not contribute while they simultaneously reap the benefits. As we will see, these practices are seen as completely despicable by the *Limningers*. This is where the line is drawn to the unacceptable tax evasion. Börje once received help from someone with a disability pension, a man deemed unfit for work and who therefore received a pension for the rest of his life:

> Once, I needed help closing a tube to a heater, I'm so bad with the plumbing. So I called one of my contacts. It was this disabled recipient who came. So he got paid by me and also got paid by the state. I only used him once, it was an emergency. So you think about this guy, how you would act yourself and then about the others. Well, it is no good. You have to pay your dues and everything. If you don't, living on social allowances and working *svart* is bloody wrong. But if you pay your dues and taxes and then take a little bit apart for yourself [it is OK]. We would not have any entrepreneurship in Sweden if it wasn't for this [possibility of cheating on dues to the state].

In this sense, the solidaristic notion of being a member of the state is vigorously alive; all citizens should provide according to their abilities, that is through their salary, to the common coffer. What you then do is up to yourself is the common understanding. At first, Börje's reasoning seems irrational. Cheating on income is presented as morally OK, whereas the other man's cheating is perceived as depraved. They both can be seen to have their fingers in the state's, and thus their common, coffer. However, Börje has put in work for which he receives payment. The whole or part of this income is taken on the side. Both the purchaser and the provider get off a bit more cheaply; they have both saved a little on this transaction by not paying the taxes due. Börje pays taxes for most of the work he does; the tax transfer is just reduced a little by his occasional *svart* job, and he contributes less money than he should to the common coffer. But the man who receives a retirement pension, for being unable to work, earns his living from the state. Even though he is not legally permitted to work, he works extra, which he should not be able to because of his retirement pension. This is morally wrong in Börje's view (cf. Frykman and Hansen 2009: 66). Needless to say, the early retired plumber certainly will have his own tales of justification. He might have been forced into early retirement, it might have been against his will and he has thus lost the possibility of a full-time wage. Those regarded as cheaters are those who have not done their fair share in contributing to society before using their free time to earn some extras. In Börje's view it is the cheating plumber who has his fingers in the coffer, Börje just puts in a bit less than he should—avoiding paying taxes on certain services he buys.

Björn offers a similar reasoning. He makes sure that he pays less than the marked price at the Chinese take-out restaurant. He claims that the meal is not officially accounted for, as the cashier at the restaurant only registers every other meal and he is not going to be overcharged and cheated. Björn did not take the initiative in this deal, but acts upon the opportunity to save a few krona. The restaurant should not benefit both from him paying the full price and then cheating on the state while not registering. The fact that in the end it is the state that loses out is not Björn's problem.

Lars is just as disillusioned with how citizens use and abuse society for their own private benefit. He told me many stories about how others grab what they need from society, and also about his involvement. The following story was one of many, and can in addition show explicitly how being involved in informally recompensed work practices is a learnt behaviour:

One thing that really bothers me was when I was employed in Gothenburg. We worked for AMU [ArbetsMarknadsUtbildning, a government-funded labour market training centre, especially for craft trades]. Well, you know from the start I was a concrete man [*sic!*]. But I am always freezing, can never keep warm. Anyway, I had to work outdoors. There is no bloody place on earth so damp and cold, really awful. Anyway, do you remember Linus Jansson? We were working at one site where it was damn cold outside and that bastard stood indoors and hammered panels and teased me. I could have killed him, I was eighteen, nineteen perhaps? So I took this extra course at AMU, to be able to work indoors. One thing led to another and one of the instructors had started a shop of his own. He was really charismatic, but damn blunt. He was a towering bloke, at least two metres tall and weighed at least 140 kg, you know, the kind of person who takes over any room he walks into. No one dared to question anything [he said or did]. So he took us out on *svart* jobs. He took the best guys, you know I was a concrete man and used to work with these things. There were also bus drivers and shipyard men, but they didn't know a thing. So he asked me if I wanted to come along. I don't remember what I got paid. But first I got travel compensation from the dole fund. Then I got paid by him, *svart* of course. It was great, super.

But there is more. We were there during this course, and when it ended I got a job with his firm. That's how he managed and made it grow. Just went in and took the guys he wanted. The other instructors had no say, maybe they got a piece as well, what do I know? Everybody who worked in his firm had been at AMU, by the way. He ran a great business, with good guys and we had fun together. Actually, it was a really good time. So we continued working for AMU and did all the jobs there. There was a lot of immigration and other stuff going on, lots of construction at this enormous centre they had in Gothenburg. So we went around, built offices, refurbished and even tore down things we had constructed ourselves. There was nil planning and too much money.

We were even at the home of the boss of the entire AMU Gothenburg and installed a bloody big oak door in his garage. He did not pay five krona for it, of that I'm certain. We built a carport for another boss, AMU paid for the materials and we were paid on the side as you say [*svart*]. We did so many reconstructions and there was so much money, and as I was already then a bit interested in how society works, I thought it was damn disgusting. Even if I was being paid, it irritated me that government money went on this! They spent so much money that finally there was a directive from above that no invoices could exceed 25,000 for refurbishment. This just resulted in a hell of a lot of 25,000 krona invoices. How bloody stupid can you be?

This is just one of Lars's many tales about having learnt to work *svart* and participate in a culture of tax cheating. His story confirms what is considered a general reason for buying *svart*—disillusionment because of public distribution of tax money. This feeling is especially ripe in this society, which it is argued is marked by a sense of equality. Lars is partly fed up with society. At one point he says: 'I just want to pay for my house; I want to be free, not having anything to do with society. That would, sometimes, feel bloody nice.' Lars's tale recounted here is yet another example of double abuse of the system. The AMU managers reap benefits from the state by having contracts and simultaneously performing such work *svart*.

Lars provides an example of when balancing does not work. The see-saw is firmly planted on the ground and the participants have left. This is the double-sided emphasis of the give and take relationship, a perceived feeling of being cheated on both the give and the take sides. Being deprived of what is rightly mine brings disenchantment and disillusion. We made acquaintance with Johan in Chap. 2. Society has treated him badly, and cheating back a little is not enough to balance the relationship. He has not much trust left in the state and instead he has more or less checked out from society.

A Fair Society

In Swedish society, where values of fairness and equality are emphasized, the *Limningers'* justifications point to situations perceived as unfair, in that some people have advantages that others do not have. For example, craftsmen have services they can exchange with each other, whereas clerks, civil servants, bureaucrats and other so-called white-collar workers have nothing to offer in return. Why should office workers or bureaucrats have to work three to four hours in order to pay for one hour formally (see also Björn's reasoning on barter in Chap. 3) when the service can instead be bought informally, making the exchange balanced and more equal? One hour for another. In the same vein, the *Limningers* reason that there are always 'others' who earn more and should therefore be able to buy everything formally, with invoices. There are many ways to find justification for a distributive side to balance the contributive side. However, voices are heard saying that, having paid the world's highest taxes, the welfare provided should be good value for money and distributed evenly.

The Pillars of Society in this chapter are those who give more than they receive. In quantitative terms we can say that they have a positive position on both the contributive side and distributive sides. They work, pay their taxes, do not use much welfare and carry a heavier load in society than most other citizens. Balance Artists have a more nuanced relation to the state and fellow citizens. If they perceive that money is wrongly spent, they make sure to get some income on the side.

A way to maintain the balance is to avoid and evade taxes when you can as some of the *Limningers* do with their involvement in *svart arbete*. But there are many other ways; where there have been demands for the transfer of provisions to those in power, there has always been more or less resistance to providing it (e.g. Laurin 1986; Isacson 1994; Pardo 1996; Roitman 2007). It has even been suggested that it is a trait almost as universal for humans as the propensity to exchange (cf. Scott 1990).

Ruben is concerned about the larger picture in society, and thinks that people in general comprehend this:

> Most people understand that they should not do it [buy services *svart*], as in the end we are all afflicted by it. But you know, well I don't know, but there is cheating in all societies. I don't think that we can say it is because we have these high taxes. It is some sort of built-in phenomenon, that it is fine to cheat the magnanimous VIPs once in a while. But I have to say that I think it is wrong.

Ruben is not the only one to emphasize the contradictions between acquiring services for private use while still caring about the larger community to which one belongs.

James Scott depicted the resistance of destitute people in societies with large differences in wealth and power. Hidden actions are a sign of resistance which has often, especially in social science, been interpreted as being directed against the public and the official. This resistance is articulated as an expression against formal relations between the weak and the powerful (Scott 1990: 13). These theories are not false, Scott argues, but incomplete, as there are many actions performed by the less powerful which contradict the official version—actions which are mostly hidden. For example, 'if it were a matter of taxes they prefer evasion instead of open tax riot' (ibid.: 86).

Can the same type of logic be applied to Swedish tax evasion? There is less in terms of social difference amid Swedes than amid the Malaysians depicted by Scott. Again, perception is key here; the *Limningers* do not see Sweden as the just society it claims to be, but rather a society where rules and regulations make it possible for the privileged to have and take additional liberties; and these inequalities are said to be increasing. In an 'equal society', this could imply that for some in privileged positions (such as Lars's boss at the AMU) are even less worthy when not contributing their 'fair share'. Being *magister* means having the upper hand. But in a society that is supposed to be based on equality, where taxpayers are treated equitably, providing *more* does not confer status. Although Swedes have greater trust in each other than many other nationalities, this does not necessarily include governmental institutions; by international comparison Swedes do not have greater trust in the judiciary to provide them with honest treatment than any other nation (Skatteverket 2006a: 217, cf. Gribnau 2015).

When the credibility of the state becomes an issue, resentment and distrust are fostered among people. This nurtures a view of actions taken by the state and its institutions as morally disputable (Pardo 2004: 11). The response of ordinary people is to use their own ingenuity, attempting to balance their reciprocal relation to the state. Paraphrases in this context are: *lura Sträng*—cheating Sträng, a former Minister of Finance; *inte skicka mer pengar till Stockholm*—stop sending money to Stockholm, the capital; *skall nåt av pengarna till Stockholm?*—is any of this money bound for Stockholm? *staten snålar*—the state is stingy; *hihi där lurade vi Ringholm*—heehee, we cheated Ringholm; *och så skall Bosse ha sitt*—and Bosse should have his share; *jag tycker vi skiter i Bosse*—we should not give a damn about Bosse. Bosse Ringholm was at the time of the interviews incumbent Minister of Finance.

So taxpayers avoid and evade taxes, in order to balance their relationship with the state. Regardless of the position they occupy in society, they have a lot to lose in expressing their resistance openly. As Hélène says, 'this is our way of protesting, even if it is a problem that we cheat some money from the state, which might need it'. This type of reasoning enforces the idea of the state as 'them', 'over there' and not 'us'. Lars situates the cheating:

> It depends on where you come from, which culture. It is probably culturally conditioned. It is wrong to steal, but not from the state. It is something we have. Maybe it is our way of protesting somehow. It has always been legitimate to steal from the state. Especially if you succeed with a [tax] deduction, then you are a star—such as with a few extra kilometres [when driving to work].[4] There is even advice in the papers on how to do it.

Most instances of buying *svart arbete* look like any other work. The same actions can be performed more or less undisclosed to the Agency, although most other people in society know about them; they are accepted. Therefore, it is a better strategy to keep transactions hidden (cf. Scott 1990: 86); they are evasive strategies rather than open protests.

CONCLUSION

If reciprocity defines the relations between exchangers and status in society, its quality is thus decided by the rules of the gift—the one obtaining too much has least status (Mauss 2002 [1990]: 11). Getting too much degrades the recipient in relation to the provider; not being able to give/ pay back creates a feeling of inferiority. Having paid 'more' gives one the upper hand in relation to the other, in which the one obtaining too much lowers his status (ibid.: 11). We have borrowed the term of being *magister* (Mauss 2002 [1990]: 95); it is a person with authority whom others look up to, and here we have used it to think about taxation in relation to ideas about a fair and equal society.

Progressive income taxation is the very definition of the Swedish contemporary welfare state. Progressive income tax means that high-income earners pay a larger share of their income in tax as they contribute more per earned krona than low-income earners do; the tax rate increases with the taxable amount. In this chapter we have seen how the *Limningers* relate to this fact in a contemporary welfare state where some continuously contribute more and others are on the receiving end. As models for different ways of engaging with the Swedish state, we have identified Pillars of Society and Balance Artists. The former see themselves as net contributors to the state whereas the Balance Artists have a more nuanced reciprocal relationship with the state and society in which they live. It could be said that they balance their dealings when they justify their *svart* dealings.

There are two sides to balancing while engaging with Mauss; it could be said to consist of reasons for giving and taking. The giving side balances what are perceived as contributions. These are feelings such as I have paid too much money, devoted too much time or conferred too much knowledge already. In short, I have given too much. It also means that others have not done their share, for example by cheating with taxes (which I, of course, have already paid). These practices are called *contributive balancing*. This is based on the reaction to a state seen as taking too high a portion of income, and takes place in opposition to the enforced collection of taxes.

The other one is the 'taking side'; the *distributive balancing*. Here, justification concerns others taking or getting too much—those not deemed deserving. Examples are politicians and bureaucrats who use money unwisely; badly, inefficiently, selectively—either for their own benefit or for a specific group of other people. Other illustrations could be citizens making claims they are not entitled to in terms of subsidies, using social insurance unjustly or claiming unemployment benefits while working (often *svart*).

There are thus different reciprocal relationships at play. Here they are the result of redistributive taxation policies and of unequal spending of tax revenue. The point is that tax policies invoke different types of reciprocal relationships; between citizens and between citizens and their state. Schumpeter's proposal, that in order to understand any society and its political life one of the best starting points is the tax system (1954), forgot one important issue. If we study a tax system in order to understand a society, it is clear that we also have to include the exchanges where taxation is avoided; not only the holes and the glitches forgotten by the tax system but how people respond to them in their everyday transactions. We have to look at both sides of reciprocity—both the positive and the negative.

Notes

1. An example of progressive marginal tax. For yearly income up to 100,000 you pay 20 per cent, for income up to 200,000 you pay 31 per cent and for income above this level is taxed at 35 per cent. A person earning 250,000 will pay income tax of 68,500 = 20 per cent × 100,000 + 31 per cent × 100,000 + 35 per cent × 50,000.
2. The notion of *Samhällsbärarna* (*The Pillars Of Society*, 1982) was first used as a title of a crime novel by Leif G.W. Persson, professor in criminology and author of many crime novels.
3. Staffan also includes other public figures outside the state administration. Their salary level is not at stake in his reasoning, but rather how they can get away with favours way out of reach for common people.
4. The kilometres Lars refers to are those you can deduct from taxes when you drive your private car for professional use.

Literature

Befu, Harumi. 1977. Social Exchange. *Annual Review of Anthropology* 6 (1): 255–281.
Björklund Larsen, Lotta. 2011. Att ge, få och ge igen. Köp av svart arbete som uttryck för medborgarens relation till staten. In *Känslan För Det Allmänna : Medborgarnas Relation till Staten Och Varandra*, ed. Kerstin Jacobsson, 237–266. Borea: Umeå.

———. 2013. Moulding Knowledge into a Legal Complex: Para-Ethnography at the Swedish Tax Agency. *Journal of Business Anthropology* 2: 209–231. http://ej.lib.cbs.dk/index.php/jba/article/view/4159

———. 2017. *Shaping Taxpayers. Values in Action at the Swedish Tax Agency.* Oxford: Berghahn Books.

de Swaan, Abram. 1988. *In Care of the State: Health Care, Education and Welfare in Europe and the USA in the Modern Era.* Cambridge: Polity Press.

Flood, Lennart. 2015. Skatter räknas, räkna med skatter. *Ekonomisk Debatt.*

Frykman, Jonas, and Kjell Hansen. 2009. *Welfare State, Health and Local Culture.* http://tryggvar.se/publikationer/welfare_state_health_and_local_culture.pdf

Gribnau, Hans. 2015. Taxation, Reciprocity and Communicative Regulation. *Tilburg Law Review* 20 (2):191–212.

Isacson, Maths. 1994. *Vardagens Ekonomi. Arbete Och Försörjning I En Mellansvensk Kommun under 1900-Talet.* Hedemora: Gidlunds.

Laurin, Urban. 1986. *På heder och samvete: skattefuskets orsaker och utbredning.* Stockholm: Norstedts.

Ledeneva, A.V. 1998. *Russia's Economy of Favours: Blat, Networking, and Informal Exchange.* Cambridge, UK: Cambridge University Press.

Lindgren, Astrid. 1976. Pomperipossa i Monismanien. *Expressen*, 10 March.

Mauss, Marcel. 2002 [1990]. *The Gift.* London: Routledge.

Pardo, Italo. 1996. *Managing Existence in Naples: Morality, Action, and Structure.* Cambridge: Cambridge University Press.

———. 2004. Introduction: Corruption, Morality and the Law. In *Between Morality and the Law: Corruption, Anthropology and Comparative Society*, ed. Italo Pardo, 1–17. Aldershot: Ashgate Pub Ltd.

Persson, Leif G.W. 1982. *Samhällsbärarna.* Stockholm: Albert Bonniers förlag.

Roitman, Janet. 2007. The Right to Tax: Economic Citizenship in the Chad Basin. *Citizenship Studies* 11 (2): 187–209.

Schumpeter, Joseph A. 1954. The Crisis of the Tax State. *International Economic Papers* 4: 5–38.

Scott, James C. 1990. *Domination and the Arts of Resistance. Hidden Transcripts.* New Haven, CT: Yale University Press.

Skatteverket. 2006a. *Purchasing and Performing Undeclared Work in Sweden: Part 1: Results from Various Studies.* Solna: Skatteverket.

———. 2006b. *Svartköp och svartjobb i Sverige. Del 1: Undersökningsresultat.* Solna: Skatteverket.

———. 2015. *Framtidens kontroll.* Solna: Skatteverket.

Slater, Don. 2002. From Calculation to Alienation: Disentangling Economic Abstractions. *Economy and Society* 31 (2): 234. Routledge. http://search.ebscohost.com/login.aspx?direct=true&db=bth&AN=6446266&site=ehost-live

Svallfors, Stefan. 1996. *Välfärdsstatens moraliska ekonomi*. Umeå: Boréa.
Thomas, Nicholas. 1991. *Entangled Objects: Exchange, Material Culture, and Colonialism in the Pacific*. Cambridge, MA: Harvard University Press. https://www.google.com/books?hl=sv&lr=&id=_HUfaBYEAOMC&oi=fnd&pg=PR11&dq=thomas+1991+anthropology+gift&ots=nlcSkmgqAc&sig=GhXODYgXbxlAr8dzAeb0l1mMw3E

CHAPTER 5

Making Tax Compliant

Abstract Taxes are repetitive exchanges that trigger taxpayers' expectations. In this sense taxation can be said to be a 'total social phenomen[on]' which, according to Marcel Mauss, has three obligations: to give, to receive and to give again. Taxes have been given—taken is perhaps more appropriate as most taxpayers do not have a choice—but there is clearly an expectation of receiving something in return. Taxation also create expectations on other members in society; that they also give and receive something back—on approximately the same level as I do. Seeing taxation as creating reciprocal relations makes for a deeper understanding of why people both comply with taxes and avoid doing so—including the everyday quid pro quo exchanges.

Keywords Balance outstandings • Fair tax share • *Quid-pro-quo* reciprocity • Fiscal citizenship

Taxation Is a Total Social Phenomenon

> Those who exchange presents with one another
> Remain friends the longest
> If things turn out successfully (Mauss 2002 [1990]: 2)

These were the lines this book started with, and so it will end. Throughout this book I have been thinking about insights from Marcel Mauss's

© The Author(s) 2018   123
L. Björklund Larsen, *A Fair Share of Tax*,
https://doi.org/10.1007/978-3-319-69772-7_5

The Gift, said to be the most inaptly named book ever in social science (Hart 2007), as it discusses so much more than an altruistic transfer of a good. *The Gift* is an armchair ethnography with examples in time and space that describe the relations created by people's various types of exchanges. Among them are the lines quoted above from the medieval Icelandic *Edda*. The great accomplishment with *The Gift* is Mauss's discovery of a mechanism that combines individual interests with the making of a social system (Douglas 2002 [1990]: xviii). Thinking about all the various types of exchange that Mauss provides us with illustrates alternative possibilities (Maurer 2016: xiv). It makes us think that there can be other ways of exchanging, other ways of organizing society as the various types of relations created by exchanges proliferate—there are many varieties of reciprocity.

If reciprocity can be used to describe any type of relation based on exchange, it probes the question of whether reciprocity as a concept has any meaning at all. There have been many who have questioned its use if it is to cover all type of exchanges, yet it is *because* of its versatility that reciprocity is forceful. It provides a strong correlation between different modes of economic exchanges; for example, when it can be used to describe both the good and the bad relations created by different types of exchanges as well as people's economic interactions with the state they reside in.

Taxes are repetitive exchanges that trigger taxpayers' expectations. In this sense taxation can be said to be a 'total social phenomen[on]', which according to Mauss has three obligations: to give, to receive and to give again. Taxes have been given—taken is perhaps more appropriate as most taxpayers do not have a choice—but there is clearly an expectation of receiving something in return. Taxation also creates expectations of other members in society; that they will also give and receive something back. This book has argued that to see taxation as creating reciprocal relations makes for a deeper understanding of why people both comply with taxes but also avoid doing so.

To understand why people pay tax does not rest on one simple explanation. This is acknowledged both by the Swedish Tax Agency and by many tax compliance researchers. Citizens do not pay tax only because they have to; they do not pay because they are treated as customers, because they believe that everybody else pays, because moral obligations demand them to share with our fellow citizens or that the tax collector is doing a fantastic job. Nor do people pay tax simply because they get something in return that is solely for their own personal benefit or because they think that the nation they reside in is utterly fantastic. It is more complicated; our willingness to pay tax depends on combinations of these factors including how tax laws are written, how these laws are interpreted and put into practice when collecting tax, but also on how this revenue is spent.

Research about tax compliance thus points to many, many explanatory factors addressing economic, legal and social issues. Some of this research has in various ways used reciprocity as a causal factor, yet in quite different ways. I proposed that there are four types of reciprocity. A *tit-for-tat* relationship expects something in return for taxes paid. This is not entirely instrumental (although it can be applied as such), but is also a strategy for giving a very clear message that I as a taxpayer expect something in return. The *copy-cat* relation's reciprocal content is in doing what others, in a similar position to me, do. If I pay my taxes so will others, and likewise if they pay so will I. Closely related to this is paying my *fair share*. If we all provide what we owe into the same treasure chest, I trust that its content will be distributed for all providers' benefit. Finally, it is a question of *equality*—of being treated in the same way as all other taxpayers, including the revenue collector. The latter has, as a governmental institute, access to an enormous amount of knowledge, and can also abuse its powerful position.

These four categories of reciprocity obviously overlap. That I desire something in return for the taxes I pay does not have to be only for my individual benefit; I might require the revenue to be spent on societal issues that I value and hold dear. Similarly, a tit-for-tat expectation can go hand in hand with all taxpayers being treated equitably and that other citizens get their fair share.

What we have seen from the Swedish example is that the everyday exchanges that create reciprocal relations between people—taxpayers—are often forgotten in tax compliance matters. Perhaps researchers are too busy concentrating on taxation from a state's perspective.[1] Such a perspective omits and forgets what citizens do every day in private—outside the realms of the state. Yet such practices also have an impact on tax compliance. It is a sort of tit-for-tat reciprocity where the state is left out of the deal. I call it a *quid pro quo* reciprocity as it does not have a vestige of a revenge element in it as the tit-for-tat varieties have. People continuously exchange for all sorts of reasons and with various intentions. They engage in market transactions, trades, barters, swaps, transfers and even thefts, making reciprocity in the sense that there is an expectation of a counteraction. In the case of avoiding tax, the point is that when the state is left out of the transaction it is often said to be owing to reciprocity. As we have seen, the *Limningers* strive for some sorts of reciprocal equilibrium when they exchange; they do so with the people with whom they exchange and it also allows them to justify their *svart* exchanges in terms of a reciprocal relation with the state.[2] On the one hand, the *svart* exchanges often take place between people who have some sort of relation; on the other hand, a *svart* trade is more justifiable if there is a perceived outstanding benefit from the state. A balance has to be struck on both counts.

In tax compliance research this latter type of reciprocity, quid pro quo, has been somewhat forgotten. Taking reciprocal relations seriously means including both people who exchange directly *and* people who exchange without including the government; it is a holistic view of people's economy, including both formal and informal exchanges. This approach makes for an increased sensitivity to what actually creates compliance in tax matters. Yes, compliance means following rules and regulations but it also means paying attention to human sociality; what it is that makes society possible.

When thinking about exchanges that ought to be subject to tax assessment, we have heard how an extended family gathers to help out painting an uncle's house; how colleagues take a few days out of their vacation to help someone refurbish her/his house, how a lamp store owner and shoe shop salesman exchanged each other's wares; how a gardener helps someone after work cutting down a tree and gets some money for his service; how a craftsman barters some bricks against a reduced invoice. According to a strict interpretation of the Swedish law all these exchanges ought to be taxed; the law says that all exchanges having value ought to be subject to tax assessment regardless of how they are remunerated. We all probably have each our view on which of the above exchanges ought to have had taxes included.

Against this background it might not be surprising that many Swedes are said to cheat with taxes. At first it might seem like a contradiction that the propensity of Swedes for purchasing *svart arbete* is quite high by international comparisons (Skatteverket 2006: 217) while they still have a great esteem for the state they live in (Inglehart and Welzel 2005). This is another reason for reciprocity being an appropriate concept to understand the somewhat idealistic view Swedes have of their relation with the state, their compatriots and society, the equitable People's Home.

BALANCE OUTSTANDING

Participating in *svart arbete* involves keeping imagined accounts with the state and other people in the community. Buying or providing services *svart* stabilizes a perceived deficit back in favour of the taxpayer. Exchanges of *svart arbete* can be made in terms of reciprocal relations when the state is perceived not to have supplied its fair share—what it should have provided as a collector of its citizens' money.

Throughout is the underlying notion of reciprocity as maintaining a balance of sorts; purchasing *svart*, valuing a service and agreeing on compensation. Viewing *svart arbete* through the spheres of community and state also highlights the tensions between the private and the public, the strong community and what services a responsible state ought to provide for its citizens, which type of exchanges ought to be subject for tax assessment and which should be left out.

As purchaser and provider in an exchange can view the transaction differently (Slater 2002: 240), so can their views on the balance of relations differ. This book calls us to take reciprocity seriously, and using ethnographic examples from Sweden I argue that the same type of expectations that exist between exchangers resides within the relationship that citizens as taxpayers have towards the state. Although exchanges between inhabitants and state are vast even from a daily perspective, impossible to quantify or account for, and immensely complicated in a welfare state, there is an abiding sense of a reciprocal relationship. From a resident's perspective, reciprocal expectations indeed have an impact on the assumptions of what society should provide. I am thus using reciprocity to look at how balancing is aimed for—a perceived equitable standing—in citizens' everyday exchanges and in how the state can find legitimate ways to tax them.

Buying *svart* can thus be seen as a response to a feeling of having contributed too much to the state. The tax level is used by many as a justification; it is said to be too high or too all-encompassing. There were many justifications such as 'I pay more than other Swedes do', with the implication that the 'others' are seen to provide less than they should. From this perspective, buying *svart* is a means of evening out other citizens' negligence in contributing fairly to the state. 'And if they cheat, I am stupid if I do not do the same.' This balancing is a model for how giving and taking, in relation to the state and towards others' contributions, ought to work. There are a number of ways in which a balance in dealings with the state can be maintained; contributions are looking at the taxpaying side—

while distributive balancing directs our scrutiny to who gets what for the collected revenue.

These views indicate that expectations and obligations are part of a citizen's relations with the state and thus also subject to reciprocal sentiments. Cheating the state via *svart* purchases is seen as taking back something which rightly belongs to me. It is a balancing act in which reciprocal relations between oneself, other residents and the state are considered.

But it is not the case that any informal purchase can be used to balance perceived outstanding debts. There is a limit, and that is when the counterpart in an exchange 'abuses' the system; s/he does not contribute to the common treasure chest while simultaneously receiving means from it—for example, by buying *svart* from a provider who is simultaneously receiving unemployment benefits while claiming to be unable to work. Such a person cheats at both ends. This is not a balancing act, but unacceptable and despicable behaviour.

FAIR SHARE—ALL NEED TO CONTRIBUTE

People have expectations that their state should provide them with services of various sorts. This book has discussed examples from Sweden, one of the richest countries in the world and organized as a welfare state that aims to supply many services for its citizens. The state therefore plays a key role in protecting and promoting the social and economic well-being of its citizens. This has not come easily and is a fairly recent accomplishment. One hundred years ago Sweden was just one of many poor countries.

Collecting the right tax by making everybody paying 'their fair share' is the Agency's strategy for building legitimacy. This fair share is neither a specific number nor a maximizing amount, but means making sure that each pays what they ought to according to the law and as democratically decided. As an old slogan from the Agency stated; *Vår åsikt om skatter ska vi uttrycka med vår röstsedel—och inte genom felaktig deklaration* (Our tax opinions should be voiced in voting, not by faulty tax returns) (Thärnström 2003: 119). Regardless of which political opinions they hold, taxpayers should obey the democratic order and pay the taxes due.

Providing such welfare is not possible, and perhaps not even wished for in many countries, and proposing a welfare state is not the subject of this book. But if there is a lesson to be learnt from the status of tax compliance in Sweden, it is that a tax collector needs to pay attention to reciprocity created by exchanges—in people's interactions with the state and its institutions but also in the manifold daily exchanges between people. Believing in reciprocity as one explanatory factor of how society is made possible, it is vital to think about how a state should tax its citizens. There are many ways in which national revenue can be organized, and in choosing taxation a government can apply many types of tax to various types of taxpayers—citizens, corporations, organizations, non-governmental organizations and so on: it must not necessarily be the people who reside and work in the nation who pay tax.

So should a nation tax citizens' income at all? Thinking of Mauss and his examples of how society is made possible by people who give, who receive and who give again, the answer is yes.

If a state taxes its citizens, it creates expectations among them. Regardless of how poor or rich you are and how little or how much tax is paid (from a macro-economic view), a taxpayer will expect something for the money paid. The amount varies between taxpayers. The point is that taxes paid create an expectation that the state will provide some benefits for the taxpayer in return.

Yet there is also the issue of a tit-for-tat reciprocity. A citizen who pays a lot needs to understand why, perhaps publicly acquiring the status of *magister* in order to keep paying.

This is Mauss's lesson; his true gift, if you like: to believe that giving something creates expectations of a countergift, which in turn triggers more giving, creating a society where we will never be quits (cf. Thomas 1991). From tax compliance research we have seen that tax revenue collected creates demands on the state, on its institutions and the people employed in various governmental capacities. Taxes paid demand a countergift of sorts.

This also means that fiscal revenue has to be treated with care. There cannot be any pilfering by corrupt officials for their private benefit and the money has to be administered with the same care as a poor person applies when being able to pay tax that is due from his/her meagre means.

One can provocatively ask if there is such a thing as citizenship without fiscal connection. Taxes paid are part of the social contract that brings rights and duties to taxpayers. Taxpayers contribute to the building of society—a material dimension of citizenship (Scholz and Lubell 1998). Throughout history the material relationship between citizens and nation states has taken on very many different guises. It has even been suggested that this is one reason why the notion of EU citizenship does not succeed (cf. Maior 2010).

There are many lessons to be learnt from reasons why people comply with their tax payments, but one very important issue to pay attention to is reciprocity. The expectation of getting something back has to be fulfilled; the *something* will be of benefit for me, my family and friends, our neighbourhood, and for services that I believe the state should provide for its citizens. Reciprocity in tax compliance is not only a tit-for-tat relationship; it is more—much more. I have to believe that my neighbour and all other citizens pay for what we should collectively share; that we can perform the everyday exchanges; that we pay according to the same rules; and that these rules are interpreted equally and fairly. Amount and tax levels will also be subjects for discussion, but it is of vital importance that we all chip in, and therefore all have expectations of getting something back. In this way are society and state maintained.

NOTES

1. One example is Godbout's claim that taxes are not gifts. According to him the state fulfils its distributive role in two diverse ways. First, through anonymous indirect or direct monetary transfers. Second, it dispenses various welfare services such as social, health, support and schools. Such provisions are not based on personal relations (Godbout and Caille 1998: 61). Yet, taking the view of taxpayers, things change, and they certainly express expectations of various sorts that can be said to have the same consequences, as Mauss pointed out in *The Gift*—reciprocity.
2. *Svart arbete*, literally black marketeering, is the informal purchase of work and thus a transaction that does not include the taxes due.

LITERATURE

Douglas, Mary. 1990. Foreword: No Free Gifts. In *The Gift*, ix–xxiii. London: Routledge.

Godbout, Jacques, and Alain Caille. 1998. *The World of the Gift*. Montreal: McGill-Queen's University Press.

Hart, Keith. 2007. Marcel Mauss: In Pursuit of the Whole. A Review Essay. *Comparative Studies in Society and History* 49 (2): 473–85.

Inglehart, Ronald, and Christian Welzel. 2005. *Modernization, Cultural Change, and Democracy: The Human Development Sequence*. Cambridge: Cambridge University Press.

Maior, Paulo Vila. 2010. European Union Citizenship: The Hard Road between a Promising Potential and Bitterness. 1415. https://ideas.repec.org/p/ufp/wpaper/1415.html

Mauss, Marcel. 2002 [1990]. *The Gift*. London: Routledge.

Maurer, Bill. 2016. Foreword: Puzzles and Pathways. In *The Gift: Expanded Edition / Marcel Mauss; Selected, Annotated and Translated by Jane I. Guyer.* ix–xvii. Chicago: HAU Books.

Scholz, John T., and Mark Lubell. 1998. Adaptive Political Attitudes: Duty, Trust, and Fear as Monitors of Tax Policy. *American Journal of Political Science* 42 (3): 903–920. http://www.jstor.org/stable/2991734

Skatteverket. 2006. *Purchasing and Performing Undeclared Work in Sweden: Part 1: Results from Various Studies*. Solna: Skatteverket.

Slater, Don. 2002. From Calculation to Alienation: Disentangling Economic Abstractions. *Economy and Society* 31 (2): 234. Routledge. http://search.ebscohost.com/login.aspx?direct=true&db=bth&AN=6446266&site=ehost-live

Thärnström, Björn. 2003. Broschyren dags att deklarera under 30 År. In *Deklarationen 100 år och andra tillbakablickar*, 119–128. Solna: Skatteverket.

Thomas, Nicholas. 1991. *Entangled Objects: Exchange, Material Culture, and Colonialism in the Pacific*. Cambridge, MA: Harvard University Press. https://www.google.com/books?hl=sv&lr=&id=_HUfaBYEAOMC&oi=fnd&pg=PR11&dq=thomas+1991+anthropology+gift&ots=nlcSkmgqAc&sig=GhXODYgXbxlAr8dzAeb0l1mMw3E

INDEX[1]

[1] Note: Page number followed by 'n' refers to notes.

© The Author(s) 2018   133
L. Björklund Larsen, *A Fair Share of Tax*,
https://doi.org/10.1007/978-3-319-69772-7

The manufacturer's authorised representative in the EU is Springer
Nature Customer Service Centre GmbH, Europaplatz 3, 69115 Heidelberg,
Germany. If you have any concerns regarding our products, please
contact ProductSafety@springernature.com

Printed and bound by CPI Group (UK) Ltd, Croydon, CR0 4YY
27/04/2026
02097627-0001